JANET MELROSE &
SHERYL NORMANDEAU

*The Prairie Gardener's
Go-To for*

Soil

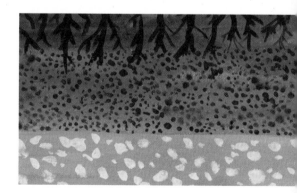

TOUCHWOOD

Copy edited by Paula Marchese

Designed by Tree Abraham

Photos by Janet Melrose and Sheryl Normandeau with the following exceptions: p. 12 (United States Department of Agriculture – Natural Resources Conservation Service), p. 15 (NatureServe / creativecommons.org), p. 102 (Marie Shark / Shutterstock.com), p. 112 (courtesy of Anne Bury).

CATALOGUING DATA AVAILABLE FROM LIBRARY AND ARCHIVES CANADA

ISBN 9781771513661 (print)

ISBN 9781771513678 (electronic)

TouchWood Editions acknowledges that the land on which we live and work is within the traditional territories of the Lkwungen (Esquimalt and Songhees), Malahat, Pacheedaht, Scia'new, T'sou-ke, W̱SÁNEĆ (Pauquachin, Tsartlip, Tsawout, Tseycum) peoples.

We acknowledge the financial support of the Government of Canada through the Canada Book Fund, and the province of British Columbia through the Book Publishing Tax Credit.

This book was produced using FSC®-certified, acid-free papers, processed chlorine free, and printed with soya-based inks.

Printed in China

26 25 24 23 22   1 2 3 4 5

Dedicated to all prairie gardeners

Introduction 7

Introduction

Soil. It's the stuff we take for granted as we walk down a forest path or across a field, or spend time digging in it.

It's the heavy, wet clay that sucks up boots in the spring, leaving you to walk home in your stocking feet. It's the silt that coats everything after a flood and dries into flat pancakes. It's the sandy stuff that dribbles through your fingers.

It's also the stuff of life.

To sustain themselves, our forefathers knew they had to care for the soil, and they did, using time-proven techniques. They loved the soil. Science has provided us, the modern gardeners, with much more knowledge about how soil works—its physical, chemical, and biological properties. We have also learned that none of these properties work in isolation. For example, your soil's pH affects its fertility, which in turn affects the soil microbes and, as a result, how our plants grow and produce for us—whether they are statuesque trees, fruit-laden shrubs, a profusion of flowers on our perennial or annual plants, or the delicious produce we grow. The soil's pH even affects the taste of what we eat! Yet that is only one example of the intricate and fascinating relationships between all the properties of soil. There are all sorts of symbiotic relationships in soil, wars fought over access to nutrients, an entire food chain of who's eating who, and who is pooping out what. In short, soil is a whole world under our feet that we are only now really getting to know and appreciate, with knowledge and controversy galore!

In *The Prairie Gardener's Go-To for Soil*, we explore a little bit of soil science so you can apply it to your gardening endeavours. We help you figure out what particles are dominant in your soil and why it's important to know this, and we give you suggestions about what you can do to ensure that the nutrients in the soil are available to your plants and not tied up underground. We dig into how to make an efficient, successful compost pile and break down the myriad of amendments that you can add to your soil so that you can make an informed decision about which ones are best for your garden. (Used coffee grounds? Eggshells? Banana peels? We even weigh in on those!) We also talk about the value of mulches and what types are well-suited for certain areas of your garden. If you're interested in trying out no-till practices, we give you some tips to get started. And we offer practical solutions to deal with problems such as compaction, heavy clay, salinity, and soilborne diseases.

Along the way, we hope that you fall in love with soil, just like we have!

—SHERYL NORMANDEAU & JANET MELROSE

Healthy soil = healthy plants!

The Nitty-Gritty

1

What is the soil food web? Why is it important?

The soil food web is a term encompassing the entire soil biology and the interactions within it. Coined by microbiologist Dr. Elaine Ingham in the late 1980s, the web allows us to easily envision the complexity of life in the soil as part of a cycle with multiple players, all feeding off each other and returning to the soil in their turn. The web expresses the entire system of soil, plants, and micro and macro life, along with the air we breathe and the water we drink, providing everything we all need to live.

The web is not like a spiderweb with all points leading into the centre; rather, it is a continuum with feedback loops. As Dr. Ingham expressed it, there are five trophic levels or zones in the energy pathway with each zone feeding into the next. Each zone has different functions.

The first trophic are the photosynthesizers, organisms that are able to photosynthesize using the pigment chlorophyll. We tend to think that plants are the only organisms that photosynthesize, but there are others just as important, such

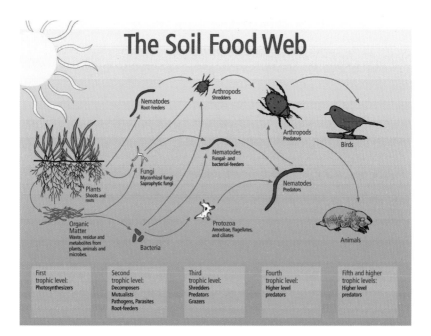

The Soil Food Web

as phytoplankton, algae, and cyanobacteria.[1] Photosynthesis creates carbon and other organic compounds, beginning the process of building organic matter.

The second trophic are largely soilborne and microscopic. They include fungi and bacteria and other organisms that decompose organic matter, liberating nutrients.[2]

The third trophic are larger organisms that eat both organic matter and members of the second trophic. In this third level are protozoa (single-celled animals), nematodes (multicellular insects with unsegmented bodies), and arthropods (invertebrate animals such as spiders, insects, and crustaceans). These organisms are predators and grazers. They live both below and above ground and shred organic matter.

The fourth and fifth trophics are higher-order predators, culminating in apex predators such as humans, who eat both plants and members of lower trophics.

It is incumbent on us to learn what a healthy soil web needs, as we are collectively dependent on it for life. Members of the second through fourth trophics are found in soil surface litter, around roots, in and between soil aggregates, and even on humus.

A healthy soil web demands that all the organisms in each trophic are present. Each must be in balance, with the right ratio of fungi to bacteria, along with a parity between predators and what they eat. Finally, nutrients must be available in forms that plants are able to uptake.[3]

A tall order, you say? Not at all, for nature has been accomplishing it without a hitch for aeons. We just need to learn how to let her get on with the job![4] —JM

Life in the Soil Food Web

TYPE OF ORGANISM	WHAT ARE THEY AND WHAT DO THEY DO?
Arthropods	Invertebrates such as insects, crustaceans, and arachnids. Many aid in the decomposition of organic matter in the soil.
Bacteria	Single-celled organisms. Most bacteria cannot photosynthesize, but some, such as cyanobacteria, can. Most bacteria in soil are decomposers of organic matter.
Fungi	Single-celled organisms. Some have fruiting forms that present as mushrooms or moulds. Some fungi help in the decomposition of organic matter. Others, such as mycorrhizal fungi, exhibit beneficial symbiosis with plant roots.
Macrofauna	Large (greater than two millimetres in size) animals that live or feed in the soil. This includes large insects such as ants and some beetles, as well as annelids such as earthworms, and molluscs such as slugs. Rodents such as mice and gophers may also be considered macrofauna.
Mesofauna	Small (between 0.1 to two millimetres in size) animals in the soil. This includes some small arthropods and worms.
Microbes	A catch-all term referring to "microorganisms," life in the soil that is too small to be seen without a microscope. This includes fungi, bacteria, and protozoa.
Nematodes	There are two main types of these tiny worms. Some live in the soil and feed on fungi and bacteria, while others parasitize animals or plants.
Protozoa	Single-celled animals, including amoebas. Many types feed on bacteria and fungi.[5]

I see the word "loam" listed in soil mixes. What, exactly, is loam?

A so-called "loamy soil" has a nearly balanced amount of sand, clay, and silt particles. It also has some organic matter in it. The ideal loam is composed of 40 percent sand and silt particles, together with 20 percent clay. This Shangri-La of loam not only contains nutrients for plants but also has the ability to hang on to them. It will retain moisture—but not too much, for too long—and it forms soil aggregates and resists compaction.

The soil textural triangle is a handy way to assess the proportions of sand, clay, and silt particles in your soil. It can help you decide your soil's type, because we certainly don't all have loamy soil! We know ours in Calgary has a goodly (badly?) amount of clay in it.

Particle size matters! Sand particles range from very fine (0.002 to 0.004 inches or 0.05 to 0.10 millimetres in diameter) to very coarse (0.04 to 0.08 inches or 1.0 to 2.0 millimetres). Silt particles have a diameter of 0.00008 to 0.002 inches or 0.002 to 0.05 millimetres. The clay particles in our Calgary gardens? Well, they have a diameter of less than 0.00008 inches or 0.002 millimetres. It's not difficult to imagine how types of soil particles can influence the movement of water and affect porosity in the soil. Bear in mind plants have different needs when it comes to soil texture. Some, like succulents and cacti, love a good sandy soil—they're not necessarily going to want loam.[6]—JM & SN

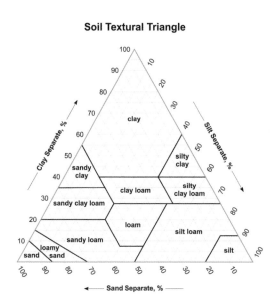

Soil Textural Triangle

15

Can I test the texture of my soil at home without paying for an expensive test?

The texture of the mineral component of soil is one of its key physical properties. Knowing the type of loam we have informs us of how to amend it to get closer to the ideal, along with influencing how we manage our soil. This knowledge can help us make better choices for beds, watering methods, plants to grow, and so on.

So, without an expensive test, how to figure out what you have? We recommend a simple method that involves getting your hands dirty!

Gather soil samples from all around your garden, from the surface to at least six inches (fifteen centimetres) deep. Mix them up in a bucket, then run it through a coarse sieve to remove debris such as rocks, bark, roots, and so forth.

Then pick up enough to fit in your hand nicely. Add a bit of water to make a ball that is just wet enough that it doesn't stick to your hand. While you are forming the ball, how does it feel? This will give you your first clues. Gritty? Sort of silky? Or slippery or sticky? Sand is gritty and coarse; silt has a smooth, silky feeling; and clay feels sticky or even slimy.

Squeeze the ball tightly, then open your hand. If it sits there holding its shape, but when you prod it gently, it falls apart, then you have loamy soil, getting close to the ideal. If the squeezed lump looks like a sausage, and you could cut it into slices, then you have a lot of clay. If it just sits there even when you poke at it, and it refuses to crumble or even change shape, then you have something approaching pottery clay. If your sample wouldn't even form a ball in the first place, you are on a beach!

Next, see if you can take your ball and squeeze it between your fingers to make a thin ribbon. The longer the ribbon, the more clay particles are present. If you have a ribbon around two inches (five centimetres) long before it breaks, then your soil sample is 20 percent clay. If your ribbon is longer still, say three, four, or more inches, your soil has even more clay particles. These ball and ribbon tests are a great way to get your hands muddy and gain hands-on knowledge of your soil![7] —JM

What is the purpose of a soil jar test?

Soil jar tests are a gardener's DIY method of determining the composition of their soil texture, expressed as percentages of the three soil particles: sand, silt, and clay.

No need for expensive equipment! All you need is a straight-sided glass jar, such as a Mason jar, water from the tap, a bit of dish soap or powder, a black felt marker, and a scoop of your garden's soil.

To start, dig down into your soil about six to eight inches (fifteen to twenty centimetres) deep to get your sample. You don't want the top layer where most of the organic matter resides.

Fill the jar about a third full with your soil sample, taking care to discard any stones and big bits such as roots and leaves. Then fill the jar with water, leaving about an inch (2.5 centimetres) of space at the top of the jar, and add one teaspoon (five millilitres) of liquid or powdered dish soap.

Shake vigorously for ten minutes until all the soil is suspended. If you have a lot of clay, you may want to use a blender for this purpose, so that your arms don't fall off. The clay particles must be properly separated from the other particles and held in suspension so they settle out last.

Then set the jar on a level surface and wait for one minute. The layer deposited during this time will be the sand and any coarser particles. With the marker, indicate this level on the jar. Then allow it to settle out for a further thirty minutes to two hours. Mark a second line on the jar where this layer stops. This is your silt layer. The water above should still be very murky with all the clay floccules still in suspension. Now leave the jar alone for two days, which will be enough time to allow all the clay particles to drop out of suspension. Draw that line on the jar with the marker. The liquid above will now be clear with perhaps a yellowish tinge. If it is still very cloudy, wait until it clears before going further.

Using a ruler, determine the depth of each layer and convert to percentages of the total depth, which, if they represent something even close to the gardener's Holy Grail of Loam, will be 40 percent sand, 40 percent silt, and 20 percent clay. To find out what you have, use the soil textural triangle diagram on page 15 and place your percentages of each along each side of the triangle to find the intersecting lines.

You now know what you have to work with and can amend your soil, so that it gets closer and closer to loam, where our plants will benefit the most from excellent air percolation, water infiltration, and available nutrients.[8] —JM

What is hard pan?

Hard pan (sometimes called plough pan) is a layer of severely compacted soil found four to thirty inches (ten to seventy-five centimetres) below the surface. Nothing can penetrate it—neither water, nor air, nor nutrients, nor plant roots. It can also lead to crusting on the soil surface and promote erosion. On the prairies, hard pan is most often found in soils with a high sodium concentration or in heavy clay soils. We have no one to blame but ourselves for hard pan: it is a problem created by the gardener or farmer. Prevent the creation of hard pan by reducing or ceasing tillage. In the spring, resist the temptation to dig around in your soil too early, when it is cold, possibly partially frozen, and wet—in a nutshell, when it is not yet workable. Build pathways into your garden for access, so you are not walking around in the beds. Finally, use cover crops (also known as green manures) wherever you can—those beautiful taproots and the organic matter the plants bring are an absolute balm for hard pan soil![9]—**SN**

What the heck is "humus"?

Humus is a mystery. Ask any group of gardeners, and chances are they won't be able to describe it. I cannot, for sure. No wonder, because scientists are not even able to agree on what it is and how it works. Lately, research has suggested humus does not even exist; that what was called "humus" was the result of chemical tests to try and figure it out some 200 years ago.[10]

That confusion is reflected in the various dictionary definitions, along with many books and other resources, not to mention loose terminology that can mean anything from topsoil to compost and a lot of other things. The best description that makes sense to me is "a large, undefinable, quite variable molecule made up of mostly carbon and hydrogen."[11]

Humus is supposedly black, stable, spongy, inert, and composed of mostly carbon. It can attract and hold on to nutrients. It also aids in soil particle aggregation. Humus has the ability to absorb and retain large amounts of water. It is generally thought to consist of large molecules, although other research suggests these molecules are actually chains of smaller molecules that form molecule conglomerates.

What is known is that humus, whatever it is and however it works, is found in healthy, fertile soils.

So, we want it, lots of it.

Leaving the matter of what exactly humus is to the scientists, what gardeners need to know about humus is that we cannot buy it, no matter what the product on sale says it is. Humus is created in situ in the garden, through the marvellous properties and processes of soil, over the course of years. The "humates" that are now available are derived from coal—not the same thing at all! There is no silver bullet for instant humus!

What we as soil regenerators can do is ensure we continually add organic matter to our soils, and allow the soil food web to take care of the rest. Then sit back, forget the confusion, and watch the action.[12] —JM

Humus-rich soils produce healthy—and, in this case, delicious and nutritious—plants.

What is organic matter (OM)? Why is it necessary? How much should I have in my soil?

Organic matter (also called soil organic matter or SOM) is very neatly defined by Dr. Fred Magdoff, professor emeritus of plant and soil science at the University of Vermont, as being "the living, the dead and the very dead." (Although Dr. Magdoff makes it clear that he did not come up with this description; it dates back a hundred years.)[13]

In a nutshell, OM comprises living and dead organisms—both plant and animal in nature—that go through a spectrum of activity to stable decay. "The living" are the soil organisms that do the work of decomposing "the dead," which are the raw materials consisting of plant debris above and below ground. Typically, these "dead" materials range from 10 to 40 percent of OM and include the annual fallen leaves, the above-ground herbaceous stems and leaves, and the roots, along with deceased soil life. The next stage is the active work of decomposition, which continues until the stable or "very dead" stage is reached. This is the magical humus, which can comprise up to 60 percent of OM.[14] It is the amount of humus that makes our soils dark, with prairie black soils having the highest percentage, down through to the grey soils of the forest regions.

Organic matter generally contains 50 percent carbon, 5 percent nitrogen, 40 percent oxygen, 5 percent hydrogen, and smaller percentages of phosphorus, sulphur, and other trace elements. It is important to note organic matter does not add new plant-available nutrients to the soil until micro-organisms die, decompose, and are recycled into the soil to be taken up by plants.

In stable and healthy soil systems, the rate of decomposition will equal the amount of OM generated annually and will ideally contain all the necessary nutrients to maintain the ecosystem. Before the prairies were settled and agriculture began, these processes were in a stable or steady state, but removal of prairie grasses has resulted in a significant reduction of OM. In urban areas where soils are disturbed more frequently, OM levels are even more affected.

Organic matter is critical to soil health as it works to improve soil structure and texture—in fact, all of soil's physical, chemical, and biological properties.

In our gardens, the goal is to attain a steady state of OM, where all that is depleted each year is replaced with an equal amount of raw materials to be degraded and recycled, creating the nutrients in our soil. Keeping our plant debris within our gardens should be our goal, whether it be the leaves that fall each autumn, the plant debris we compost and return, or the mulch that slowly disappears into the soil. How much is enough? Well, the black soil of the prairies historically had between 6 to 10 percent OM. That seems an excellent percentage for gardeners to aspire to![15]—JM

Autumn leaves can help make up the OM in our soil.

What is the rhizosphere? Why is it so important?

Way back in 1904, a German agronomist and plant physiologist, Lorenz Hiltner, identified a zone surrounding roots that was positively teeming with unique micro-organisms. This zone was named the rhizosphere, from the Greek *rhiza*, meaning "roots."

Hiltner discovered a thin (only 0.07 to 0.11 inches or 2 to 3 millimetres thick) area surrounding roots where microbes were up to 1,000 to 2,000 times more concentrated, assisting with both nutrient uptake by the roots and, most interestingly, protection from pathogens. In this zone, plants secrete a number of organic compounds called rhizodeposits, injecting carbon into the soil, which is then eagerly consumed by the microbes. These rhizodeposits are in the mucilage, surrounding the root tips of plants, easing their way through the surrounding soil as they search for moisture and water. They are in the root exudates, released by the plant to attract specific types of bacteria and fungi. They also labour to change the chemical and physical properties of the surrounding soil and even work to deter competing roots from getting too close.

All that microbial action, as well as nutrients being released and attracted, results in a distinctly different environment, with a lower pH, higher amounts of organic matter and carbon dioxide (CO_2), and lower amounts of soil nutrients and water as these substances flow in and are taken up by the roots of plants and soil life. Even more interesting, there are fewer contaminants present. All that action results in a lot of dead microbes too, with all the nutrients in their bodies now available for uptake. Enzymes contained in both the soil life and the roots are released upon death; thus, these enzymes are responsible for a lot of the chemical reaction in cells. The enzymes work to degrade organic matter and other enzymes and are absorbed by the soil and other microbes. Each plant's rhizosphere will be different, reflecting its needs, and each garden will have a different rhizosphere, as its individual plants respond to the climate and soil composition.

Protecting the rhizosphere in our gardens means we should strive to do no harm, be it by tilling or uprooting plants unnecessarily. It requires soil moisture be kept at as consistent a level as possible; a drought will cause the microbial population to decrease abruptly, upsetting the balance, and when they rebound with a flood of moisture, they will draw on nutrients heavily, causing a lack of nutrients to be available to plants. Any pesticide, organic or synthesized, applied to plants has the potential to alter or damage the rhizosphere.

We are always told that it isn't a good idea to disturb plant roots. Now we know why in broad strokes. Research on the rhizosphere keeps turning up more and more fascinating interactions between plants and soil life. While they aren't sentient in the way animals are, they certainly know their business![16]—JM

This section of exposed rhizosphere is teeming with microscopic life.

What are mycorrhizal fungi, and how are they beneficial to my garden?

Mycorrhizal fungi, literally from the Latin *myco* (fungi) and the Greek *rhiza* (root), are groups of fungi that form symbiotic relationships with plants for the mutual benefit and the survival of various species from different kingdoms.

Fossil evidence dating back some 400 million to 500 million years speaks to these relationships forming, as plants first established themselves on dry land. Without roots as yet, those protoplants needed the fungi to source water and nutrients. These relationships have evolved and strengthened through the aeons as both plant and fungal life developed. In the millions of fungus species, there are some 6,000 species of mycorrhizal fungi.[17]

It wasn't until the 1880s that Polish scientist Dr. Franciszek Kamieński discovered this symbiotic relationship, focusing on earlier observations that had been made of the roots of plants being literally bound together by the hyphae (filaments) of fungi. Though it was thought at first to be a parasitic relationship that harmed plants, Dr. Kamieński determined the absolute necessity of this relationship for plants to be able to thrive. Originally it was believed that only a few species from each kingdom formed these relationships, but we know now that upwards of 90 percent of all plants have these symbiotic relationships. Some are so specialized, only a single plant species will interact with a single species of fungus. Some are generalists, and luckily for today's gardeners and their gardens, the generalists are in the majority, which works in our favour since we bring in an array of plant species to our gardens.

Only two types of mycorrhizal fungi contain the majority of species, which are the ones we commonly have in our gardens. Endomycorrhizae, the largest group, are able to enter into root cells and create exchange structures (arbuscules). The other group, ectomycorrhizae, which mostly work with evergreens and hardwood trees, develop sheaths around roots and create exchange structures called Hartig nets. Both exist within the rhizosphere, and their hyphae seek out nutrients and moisture far and wide, literally going into and between soil particles where, due to their size, no root is able to go. While roots do seek out and can absorb nutrients and moisture, it is these fungi that do the heavy lifting and make it all

Seeing mushrooms in your garden?
They are a sign that your soil is healthy.

possible. The fungi both increase a root's biomass and extend the area roots can reach by up to fifty times.

Plants will direct upwards of 20 percent of the carbohydrates formed through photosynthesis down into the soil to be available to the fungi and the rest of the microbial life. In return, the fungi convey both water and nutrients to the plant. But the relationships may go beyond those benefits as plants may have more than one relationship at the same time. Other mycorrhizal fungi will act to prevent pathogens from entering the roots. Their presence also aids a plant's stress tolerance to drought, heat, salinity, and soil contaminants.

The good news is any well-established garden with healthy soil has massive numbers of mycorrhizal fungi present. Every so often we will be alerted to their (and other fungi's) presence by their fruiting bodies, sent up to disperse spores far and wide to colonize other soils. We call them mushrooms and should celebrate their fleeting occurrence as evidence that all is well in the soil and with our plant roots.[18] —JM

If earthworms are in the soil, does that mean it is healthy?

As earthworms consume soil and the organic matter it contains (think of delicious things like compost, rotted manure, and decomposing grass clippings), they break it down in their gut, which contains multitudes of beneficial organisms. Their gizzards work to physically grind the material up using muscle contractions. Worms don't have the most efficient digestive systems, but their excretions, called worm castings, are chock full of good microbes, partially digested plant matter, particles of soil, and nutrients. All those microbes continue to work after they've exited the tubular tracts of the worms, and the decomposition process of organic matter continues naturally after the worms have wiggled onto new territory. It is estimated that the number of active microbes present in worm castings is up to twenty times higher than in regular compost!

Every little bit counts when it comes to providing goodness for your soil, so if you see earthworms in your garden, you know that something is going right. They are content with the amount of organic matter in your soil, and they are happily ploughing around and making your soil better. Research has shown that earthworms are capable of producing an incredible 700 pounds (317 kilograms) of castings per acre (0.4 hectares).

Earthworms also create tunnels as they munch and move their way through the soil. These tunnels open up spaces in the soil, facilitating the movement of water and air. Compacted soil particles are loosened, offering better drainage. You know what that translates into: happier plants with stronger root systems.

Although they are industrious little creatures, one place where their efficiency and helpfulness are not welcome is in the forest. All the things we love them for in our gardens can actually change forest ecosystems—and not for the better! Nearly all of the earthworm populations in Canada are non-native, having been brought here hundreds of years ago by early European settlers. It turns out the speed at which large populations of earthworms break down nutrients from fallen leaves and other decomposing plant matter is a little too quick and dirty for many plants that grow in forests, which rely on the consistent, slow release of natural decay. There are no gardeners to go out and replenish the organic matter, so the trees and shrubs and understorey plants do not have a continuous source of new nutrients to draw from. Earthworms can also digest seeds and do not deposit them whole like birds and many mammals, which ruins the chances of germination for some unlucky plants. And those tunnels that the worms are famous for making? They force the forest soils to drain too quickly, leading to issues with erosion and runoff. The tunnels also interfere with the symbiotic relationship between fungi and plants in the forest, which can have repercussions on plant growth.

Over time, the culmination of all of these detrimental effects can decrease the diversity of native plants in the understorey of our forests. Studies now show that all over North America, this quiet wiggly earthworm is altering our forest ecosystems.[19]—SN

Earthworms can help promote good soil structure and reduce compaction in our gardens.

What does "soil tilth" mean, and why is it important?

Tilth is a way of describing the physical condition of soil and how it influences plant growth. If your soil is "in good heart," so to speak, it's going to be just right for seeds to germinate in, offering you the ability to sow them at the correct depth and the opportunity for good seed-to-soil contact. (Have you ever tried to sow seeds in compacted soil? Not fun!) Good tilth allows roots to develop properly and spread, which means they can take up nutrients and water. Your plants are going to thrive, not merely survive. Soil with good tilth has a balance of soil aggregates and both small and large pores, ensuring there is sufficient drainage, with no oxygen deficiency. Compaction isn't an issue with soil that has good tilth, and the availability and movement of nutrients for plants to take up is not inhibited.

How do you obtain this much-desired good tilth?

* Reduce or stop tilling
* Let soil micro-organisms do their work
* Add organic matter as needed (yes, that means compost!)
* Rotate crops
* Use cover crops

Easier said than done, I know, but taking up the challenge will be worth it in time![20] —SN

What do I have to do to get well-draining, moisture-retentive soil?

It all comes down to understanding the water-holding capacity of your soil. This is the amount of water that soil can hold for plant use. If your garden beds have completely maximized their water-holding capacity, they are said to have reached field capacity. That means the addition of any more water will lead to runoff and possibly flooding.

Water-holding capacity is influenced by soil texture and the amount of organic matter the soil contains. The fine, small silt and clay particles in soil actually have a larger surface area in the soil as they are less porous and more tightly packed together. That means they can hold more water than sand, which has large particles and pores that water drains freely out of. When it comes to your soil, you want to have your cake and eat it, too! The water should drain, but not too quickly, because your plants need that moisture. Organic matter in the soil increases the water-holding capacity, so if your soil is percolating way too fast, additions of amendments such as compost may help achieve the balance you want. (On the opposite spectrum, organic matter can also help reduce the compaction sometimes found in clay soil and, over the long term, can prevent puddling.) Practising minimal or no-till gardening may also promote better water-holding capacity.[21] — SN

This isn't an example of localized flooding, but rather effects of the catastrophic overland flooding that occurred in Calgary in June of 2013. It illustrates — in an extreme way — how soil that cannot drain is affected by water. (Silt has also been deposited here.)

Does the pH of my garden soil matter?

Power of hydrogen (pH) is one of the most important chemical properties for gardeners to understand as it expresses whether our soils are acidic, neutral, or alkaline. The property pH isn't a measure of fertility of soil, but it has a very large effect on how nutrients are held in the soil and made available to plants. It turns out that pH also affects levels of soil bacteria, nutrient leaching, toxicity in soil, and even soil structure![22]

Hydrogen ions (H^+) and hydroxyl ions (OH^-) exist in the soil solution (a film of water with dissolved gases, minerals, and organic matter). Measuring the pH indicates the concentration of the ions on a logarithmic scale from 1 to 14, with 7 being neutral, when both the positive and negative ions are in balance. A greater concentration of hydrogen ions (H^+) reduces pH, making soils acidic. The lowest measure is the equivalent of vinegar. On the other end of the spectrum, a greater concentration of hydroxyl ions (OH^-) increases alkalinity with the extreme end being the equivalent of baking soda.

Most of our plants grow best in soils that are fairly neutral, ranging from 5.5 to 8. In that range, soil nutrients are not bound tightly to the ions and are readily available in the soil solution, especially the macronutrients of nitrogen, phosphorus, and potassium, as well as sulphur.

In acidic soils, nutrients such as phosphorus, calcium, and magnesium are less available, while others such as manganese and aluminum can reach toxic levels. Highly acidic soils are largely deficient in nutrient availability.[23]

Alkaline soils, on the other hand, also tightly bind phosphorus, along with iron, manganese, boron, copper, and zinc, as well as many other trace elements. On the prairies, where alkaline soils dominate, we often see interveinal chlorosis (the yellowing between the veins on leaves), which is due to iron not being available.[24]

Gardeners need to know the pH of their soils to determine how best to amend them so that the nutrients we add will end up in our plants and will not be held in the soil. Simple tests are available in most garden centres, though they are really not sensitive enough to give precise information. There are other more extensive tests that involve collecting soil samples and sending them off to laboratories for a full analysis.

The native soil in any area is strongly influenced by the underlying parent rock. Trying to amend a soil's pH is challenging as soil will always want to revert back to its natural state. Compost and other organic matter does work to buffer the pH of any soil, allowing nutrients to be more readily available, no matter which side of neutral your soil is on. To be honest, I never bother with trying to seriously change the pH of my soil, as I view that this is the soil that I have (so long as it is healthy), just like most folks accept that they have straight or curly hair. If you strongly desire to amend your soil's pH, you have to make it an ongoing affair and know that you may not succeed.—JM

I want to grow rhododendrons or blueberries or other plants that love acidic soil. How do I alter the pH of my soil to suit them?

Prairie soils tend to be alkaline, so it may be likely that acidification for these specific plants is necessary, but to be sure, do a soil test first. There is no point amending soil if it is already hospitable to what you want to plant. If you have only a few plants that need acidic soil, don't bother with amending the whole flower bed—that doesn't make sense, either. In such a case, use a fertilizer that also acidifies, and simply apply it to the plants that require it.

If you need to acidify a large area of soil, you have a few options. Contrary to popular belief, peat moss doesn't do the best job of acidifying soil—you need a lot of it to see results (four to six inches or ten to fifteen centimetres, dug into the topsoil). Frequent reapplications are necessary, but at least it is inexpensive to purchase. Bear in mind there is some debate as to the sustainability of peat moss and the environmental impact of its harvest (see pages 82–83).

Evergreen needles will acidify the soil only if they are fresh (green), but the results are not dramatic. The brown ones are good for mulch, but not to alter pH. You will need to collect so many fresh evergreen needles to accomplish the task that you won't even want to look at an evergreen tree afterwards, and (groan!) reapplication will be frequent. That old myth that evergreen needles are super acidic needs to be tossed out once and for all.

Vinegar is often touted as a soil acidifier on the internet. Don't believe everything you read on the internet. Applying straight vinegar will damage and burn your plants.

Aluminum sulphate is commonly used to acidify soil, as well as to treat symptoms of iron deficiency. When applying aluminum sulphate, follow the instructions on the package label to a T—you need a lot of it to work, but overapplying it is a terrible idea.

Elemental sulphur is the other recommended option for acidifying soil. It takes a long time to work, and you may need to apply it over successive years, but once you reach the required pH, you won't have to reapply it for a long time. It is best to dig elemental sulphur in before you plant, as it doesn't work very well as a side-dressing for existing plantings.

Don't forget to re-test! Conduct a soil test every three years to see if it is necessary to replenish amendments for acidification.[25] — SN

Evergreen needles aren't as acidic as commonly believed.

What are nutrient deficiencies in soil?

Plants need several types of elements in varying quantities to grow and reproduce. The exact number of them depends on the source of your information—alas, scientists and gardeners have not reached a consensus on this topic!

For our purposes in this book, I'm noting three macronutrients, three secondary nutrients, and seven micronutrients as the keys to plant life. (You're going to see others on lists found elsewhere, including nickel, sodium, fluorine, and iodine. Some are categorized as beneficial elements, not essential ones—often because only specific plant species use them. Cobalt and silicon are examples.) Macronutrients, which are essential for plant development and overall health, include nitrogen, phosphorus, and potassium. Calcium, magnesium, and sulphur are considered secondary nutrients. Micronutrients such as boron, chlorine, copper, iron, manganese, molybdenum, and zinc are also needed for plant growth, but

This bean seedling appears to be suffering from a combination of nitrogen deficiency and insufficient water.

they are used by plants only in small quantities. Micronutrients are generally not deficient in most soils, but they may not be available for plants to take up, which makes it appear as though a deficiency is the issue.

The mobility of nutrients in the soil and within plants themselves is part of the key to availability. Some nutrients are highly water soluble and more mobile than others—many forms of nitrogen are in this category. Quite often, maintaining a regular watering schedule will greatly promote nutrient availability.

Sometimes when one nutrient is tied up or missing in soil, it can influence the function of another nutrient. For example, if there is too much magnesium in your soil, you may see an accompanying deficiency in calcium and potassium . . . and if there is too much potassium, magnesium may not be available to plants to use. Everything is truly connected!

Remember, too, that issues like yellowing of foliage and weak stems may not necessarily be caused by nutrient deficiencies. Disagreeable environmental conditions, pests, diseases, and poor cultivation practices may all cause a plant to look unhealthy. The only real way to determine if you have a nutrient deficiency in your soil is to do a soil test, and possibly a plant tissue test. The laboratory doing the testing will make recommendations for corrections, if needed. If the soil food web is in decent working order, and you are regularly amending your soil with organic matter, nutrient deficiencies shouldn't be something you have to deal with too often.[26]—SN

When should I have my soil tested? Is it okay if I use a home kit? What do commercial companies test for?

There are a few important reasons to do a soil test. The most common one is to determine if your soil is deficient in nutrients and, if so, which ones require correction. Soil tests can also evaluate factors affecting the availability of nutrients to plants. They can test for pH, cation exchange capacity (CEC), and salinity. As well, if you suspect that the soil in your garden has been contaminated with metals or other substances, a soil test is necessary before you plant.

Inexpensive home testing kits are available at most garden centres and many big-box stores. They usually only test soil pH and NPK (nitrogen, phosphorus, and potassium) levels; they do not test other nutrients, nor check for contaminants. You will not receive recommendations regarding amendments if the soil is found deficient in nutrients. However, if you want to know a few basics about your soil, these kits are suitable.

A soil testing laboratory provides a much more detailed and reliable report than any home testing kit. It can be difficult to track down a lab in your area, however, as most do not provide residential services, but rather agricultural or industrial testing. Before you rush out into your garden and scoop up soil samples, phone around and inquire about what types of tests your local labs can do and what they charge for their services.

The lab will give you directions on how to take proper soil samples, but generally you will take samples from several areas of your yard: near trees and shrubs, and near your edible and ornamental garden beds. The samples should be taken four to six inches (ten to fifteen centimetres) below the surface. Use a wooden or plastic spoon to put the soil in a plastic bag, as some metals will contaminate the samples. Most of the time, the lab will have you mix the samples, but confirm that before you send it in.

The lab will then combine the soil with water and either an alkaline or acidic extract, which will free up the nutrients for analysis.

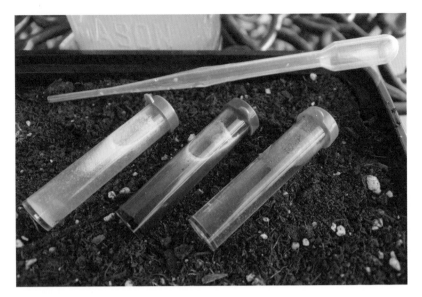

A home soil test kit can offer a basic analysis of the pH of your garden soil, as well as the macronutrients it contains.

Some labs will do more specialized biological testing on plant tissues, which can tell you more about how much of the nutrients in your soil is actually reaching your plants. Micronutrients can be successfully measured this way. The only issue with plant tissue analysis is that it can't tell you *why* nutrients aren't available to your plants—you have to figure that out yourself.[27] —SN

One of my plants has been killed by a soilborne disease. Can I plant something else in the same place?

The list of common soilborne pathogens is lengthy and features some of the usual suspects including *Rhizoctonia* spp., *Fusarium* spp., *Verticillium* spp., *Sclerotinia* spp., *Pythium* spp., and *Phytophthora* spp. These pathogens are responsible for costly losses in commercial agriculture worldwide, but they also show up from time to time in our home gardens. If you've ever had a seedling dampen off due to fusarium, you know what I'm talking about. It's heartbreaking enough if it's a tray full of seedlings that have succumbed to a soilborne pathogen, but what if it's a beautiful mature tree in your backyard? Soilborne pathogens can cause a range of problems, including root rot, yellowing of foliage and stems, twig or branch dieback, and stunting or deformation of plant tissues. The pathogens may overwinter in soil, and some may persist for years. As well, they may stick around regardless of whether the host plant is still present. Remember, too, that in order for the so-called "disease triangle" to function successfully, environmental conditions must be just so for the pathogens to infect the host plant.

Meticulous sanitation practices are needed to combat soilborne disease. Clean up all plant debris from the diseased plants. If you need to prune away diseased tissue, sterilize your tools, and properly dispose of the plant wastes (not in your composter!). Don't let weeds encroach on the plants that are sick—the pathogens may spread to the weed plants as well. When you water, try to prevent moisture from splashing up into the foliage of the diseased plant, as it may spread spores around.

If you have to remove the diseased plant, there is no need to sterilize the soil afterward. You will, however, need to carefully consider what to plant in its place. Select a plant that is not a host of the same pathogen (just in case it is still lingering in the soil), or choose a cultivar that has been bred specifically for resistance to soilborne diseases.

Finally, there is evidence to suggest that adding organic matter such as compost to your soil will encourage heightened microbial activity that can crowd out and suppress soilborne pathogens. It can't hurt to give it a try.[28]—SN

What is a good growing medium mix to use in raised beds?

As with growing medium mixes for containers, you have umpteen options. Whatever you use should have plenty of aeration, have the capacity to hold water, and drain well. If you are using a mix containing soil, it should have good tilth (think beautiful soft crumbs!). Amendments such as worm castings are always welcome additions.

EASY-PEASY RAISED BED GROWING MEDIUM MIX

* 1 part topsoil
* 1 part compost
* 1 part peat moss or coir (coconut fibre) —SN

As Janet always says, grow with a medium that has oomph!

What kind of growing medium should I put in containers?

There are as many "recipes" for container growing medium as there are for chocolate chip cookies. Well, perhaps not quite . . .

There are a few key things to remember. Do not use soil straight from your garden beds in containers, unless you want a compacted, heavy mass that resembles concrete. Plant roots cannot go anywhere in soil like that, so avoid it at all costs. If you need any more reasons to keep garden soil in the in-ground beds, think about the weed seeds and pathogens it may carry. Not appealing in the least. That soil belongs in the ground.

The growing medium you need for containers should hold moisture but not contain too much clay. In what seems like a contradiction, but is not, it also needs to drain, so it shouldn't have an overabundance of sand. Aeration is a must for those roots to stay healthy. It's a tall order but not that difficult to achieve.

BASIC SOILLESS CONTAINER MIX

* 1 part peat moss or coir
* 1 part perlite or vermiculite

BASIC SOIL-BASED CONTAINER MIX

* 1 part topsoil
* 1 part peat moss or coir
* 1 part perlite or vermiculite

This soilless container mix is ready to be planted!

Because these mixes do not offer any nutrients, you need to add them. Compost or worm castings are excellent choices, but a few handfuls of various meals won't hurt either. If you are starting seeds or growing seedlings in your mix, hold off on the amendments until they are old enough to handle them.

And, remember, tailor the mix the way you want to—don't be afraid to experiment! You'll get to know the exact feel and look of the type of mix you want, and you'll see how your plants respond to it.[29] —SN

What is a water infiltration test? How do I do it?

A water infiltration test (often called a percolation test) is conducted when you want to find out how quickly water enters the soil. Soil has the capacity to hold water, but if water runs too quickly through soil particles, it is an indicator there isn't a lot of organic matter in the soil storing the water for later use. If the water pools too much, issues with runoff and erosion can occur. You're looking for something in between!

Find a bare patch of soil in an area you want to test. If you have the desire to spend the money, you can actually purchase a measuring tool called an infiltrometer, but in a pinch, you can simply dig a hole six to twelve inches (fifteen to thirty centimetres) deep and six inches (fifteen centimetres) in diameter. Place a large tin can with both ends removed into the hole. Then jam a ruler into the hole, putting the end with the lowest measurements into the hole. (Make sure the ruler is large enough to reach the top of the hole.) Fill the hole with water, then wait for a few hours. This will saturate the soil. Refill the hole with water, then wait for another hour or two. Make sure you're keeping track of the time! Measure the depth of the water in the hole and do a little math. If your soil is composed of primarily sand particles, the water will move through the soil at a rate of 1 to 8 inches (2.5 to 20 centimetres) per hour. For silt, that number drops to 0.1 to 1 inch (0.25 to 2.5 centimetres) per hour, and for clay, 0.1 inches (0.25 centimetres) or less per hour. Now you have some indicator as to the predominant types of particles in your soil, and you can determine if you should add any amendments. (Dare I say that compost should be one of them?)[30] —SN

What does it mean when I see a white crust on my soil?

A white crust on top of the soil is an indicator of high salinity or, in other words, a concentration of salts. The salts can originate from different sources, including irrigation water and fertilizers. Salinity can result in spotty germination and poor plant growth and may potentially reduce yields in edible crops. In some cases, natural rock deposits hold high salt concentrations, and when groundwater flows through the formations, it carries the salts with it. Seepage brings the salts to the surface of the soil, where they collect.

Fixing soil salinity is tricky unless you are dealing with plants grown in containers. Saline soils in containers may be flushed out with water to remove the excess salts. You need quite a bit of water to accomplish this leaching process—for example, for a 1-gallon (3.78-litre) pot, 2 gallons (7.6 litres) of water is recommended. Pour the water into the pot, and let it run out of the drainage holes at the bottom of the pot. It may seem nerve-racking—isn't it a bit too much water?—but it is a fairly quick way to deal with the problem. If leaching doesn't seem to solve the issue, repot your plant into fresh soil and a new container.

With in-ground beds, preventing and dealing with saline soils requires a multi-pronged approach:

* Improve soil drainage by adding amendments of organic matter such as compost
* Don't overfertilize
* Incorporate cover crops into your regular gardening practices
* Minimize or eliminate tilling[31] —sn

Take the tighty-whitie test

Here is a simple and eloquent, not to mention fun, test to learn about your soil's organic matter content and its microbiology. The premise is that microbes need organic matter to survive, never mind thrive.

To do the test, first weigh a pair of men's underwear and record the measurement. The briefs must be entirely cotton except for the elastic band. Lay them into a soil trench about two inches (five centimetres) deep, then cover them up with soil, and wait five weeks. (Don't forget where you buried them!) When the prescribed time has elapsed, dig the underpants back up again, and you will see how much of the undergarments have been consumed. Almost gone? You, or rather your soil, is gold! Bottoms still almost intact? You have a lot of work to do to improve your soil's organic matter content! To get a more specific measure of how much of the tighty-whities was consumed, weigh them again. If they weigh less than half of the original weight, your soil is tops, but if only 20 percent or less has been consumed, get back to work!

This test was the brainchild of the South Dakota Soil Health Coalition's first Soil Health School back in 2016, and the results were astonishing.

We dare you to sacrifice a pair of tighty-whities![32]—**JM**

Compost

2

What is the difference between hot and cold composting?

All organic matter, be it animal, plant, or microbial, decomposes naturally over time. Composting is nothing more than attempting to provide ideal conditions for this process to occur faster or more efficiently in an easily managed way.

Compost then is primarily plant-based, partially decomposed organic matter. It is often a dark brown, almost black, earthy-smelling substance that is a terrific soil conditioner. Gardeners call it "black gold" for good reason.

Composting requires four things: oxygen, water, space, and materials. The generally accepted amount of space needed is at least a four-by-four-foot (one cubic metre) enclosure. Various materials, from wood to metal, can be used to make your bin. They can be purchased already constructed or they can be DIY versions. It's key to have access to work the materials in the bin and enough volume so the composting process can occur efficiently. The microbes, insects, and worms that do the work are all aerobic organisms, so there needs to be availability of oxygen. Likewise, moisture is required, with the pile being consistently moist or damp, but not wringing wet.

Place your compost pile where it will receive some sun, but more important is not having it in a low spot of the garden where it will become too wet. Even more crucial is having it in the working area of the garden! When building your compost pile, layer materials, alternating browns and greens, and water each layer as you go to get moisture inside right away. You may also want to put a cover on it to prevent it from being waterlogged in heavy rains.

There are a couple of different methods to making compost, and the choice you make depends on the amount of effort you want to exert, how quickly you want compost, how much space you have, and the type and volume of plant waste you want to compost.

Hot or active composting will produce compost in a relatively short time as you are actively working the materials by turning them over and aerating. You will also need a compost thermometer. Once you build your pile, you insert the compost

This is a great set-up to create compost for your garden.

thermometer and wait for the action to kick in. Initially fungi are the most active, but after nitrogen is released, bacteria take over and start releasing heat. When the thermometer reads 130°F (55°C), turn the pile, bringing the outside materials into the middle. The pile will cool down, and a different bunch of fungi and bacteria will take over with heat reaching 130°F (55°C) again or possibly 160°F (70°C) when thermophilic bacteria enter the picture. I am always astonished at the heat that is generated! Turn the pile over again, bringing those outside materials back in again. Then let everything settle down, and allow the microbial populations to build back up and "finish" the compost. The whole process takes from two to six months, depending on weather and how well you manage the process.

Cold or passive composting involves building your pile, usually in layers of greens and browns (see pages 56–57), then simply leaving it be, except for watering it occasionally so that it is consistently damp. It helps to build your pile with a base of some decaying wood, branches, and twigs to aid in aeration and drainage. The microbes and other organisms will do their thing, and over time the materials will decompose, except for the outside of the pile, which can be used to build another one in due course. The pile will gently heat up to 130°F (55°C), then cool down, but it will take more time to complete the process. I typically give my passive compost bins a full year and take them apart in the fall, sieve the compost out, and use the remainder to start the next one.

While cold composting takes longer, the bonus is a great biodiversity of soil life, as the organic matter is left undisturbed while decomposition occurs. The downside is that pathogens, insect eggs, and weed seeds will not be killed off in the process, lacking the thermophilic temperature reached with hot composting, so you have to be a bit more careful with what materials you use. I used to have a lot of trouble keeping the pile moist enough as I would forget to water consistently. My remedy is to add a layer of soil on top of the pile and plant my squash plants in it. I get great squash, and the pile gets regularly watered to boot!

Compost is considered a soil amendment, not fertilizer, as the nutrients it contains are variable, almost entirely dependent on the materials that began the process. The old saying "Garbage in, garbage out" is apt for compost, too. The results are also variable, depending on the care and attention you gave your compost pile. But done properly, the results are that "black gold" gardeners exult over.[1]—JM

In this twist on trench composting, throwing squash seeds into your compost pile can sometimes yield surprising volunteers!

Should I bury my veggie waste directly into the garden?

Known as trench or pit composting, or in a still smaller form as "dig and drop" composting, this type of composting has a lot of benefits and not many downsides.

Sometimes called "lazy man's composting," it removes the work of managing an aerobic composting system, including watering, aerating, and finally turning the finished product into the garden. Done properly, it won't attract visitors such as rodents and wasps that can make their homes in compost bins, nor will there be the possibility of unsavory aromas. It also has the real benefit of placing small amounts of organic matter adjacent to plants, where it can be speedily converted to nutrients that are then available to plants as they need them throughout the season.

The downsides are that it cannot be done in winter, and you have to be very careful to not disturb plant roots. You should also not use any material that might be used in a hot composting system, such as weeds gone to seed or diseased plant waste. If done in an annual garden, you should wait up to six weeks for the material to decompose thoroughly before sowing or transplanting in young seedlings, or have a garden bed that you leave fallow for this use. If you are planning to do this system in the dig-and-drop style between rows already planted, you will need to leave at least 1 foot (0.3 metres) between the rows, which means that area of your garden will not be available for plants. Some gardeners alternate the composting and planting areas every other year, giving the organic matter a full year to break down. (This timeline is also suitable for a raised bed.) Others use a more involved three-year cycle with an organic-mulch pathway, a row for growing plants that season, and a composting trench. Each of these areas rotates each year, so that the organic matter has additional time to break down. It is considered a slower method than traditional active composting, as you are not aerating, but seeing as you don't have to tend it at all, that seems to be a pretty good trade-off.

To do trench composting, simply collect your kitchen waste in a pail and, when ready, dig a trench that is around twelve inches (thirty centimetres) deep, either between rows in an already growing bed or in fallow space where nothing is growing. Add four to six inches (ten to eighteen centimetres) of kitchen waste and replace the soil you removed. Then wait while the soil life does the work, and start collecting a new pail of kitchen waste![2] **—JM**

53

What does the carbon-to-nitrogen ratio mean?

Organic matter is composed of carbon and nitrogen, but of course, not all OM is the same, so the quantities of carbon and nitrogen vary. In a compost bin, that quantity matters, as the types of microbes that actively decompose those materials have certain preferences, and your compost pile will break down far more efficiently if you meet their requirements. Research has shown the microbes in your compost bin love a ratio of 30:1 (carbon to nitrogen). For comparison, here are the C:N ratios of some common materials you might put into your composter:

* Dried leaves: 60:1
* Shredded newspaper: 175:1
* Sawdust: 325:1
* Straw: 75:1
* Grass clippings: 20:1
* Manure: 15:1
* Vegetable scraps: 25:1
* Coffee grounds: 20:1

As you can see from this list, if you put pieces of carbon-rich shredded newspaper or bucketfuls of sawdust in your compost bin, you had better throw in some nitrogen-rich grass clippings or vegetable scraps as a chaser. Don't stress out too much about these numbers, though—the goal is to get a mix of materials, and understand if you put too much of one type of material in the bin, you will need to offset it.[3] —SN

*Vegetable wastes make good "greens"
for your compost.*

What types of wastes should I put into my composter?

On page 54 we talk about the carbon-to-nitrogen ratio, which is key for successful composting. Carbons are commonly designated as "brown" materials and nitrogen-based materials are "green." To help you figure out the ingredients you need to get that C:N ratio working for your own compost bin, here is a breakdown of commonly composted items, divided into those two categories:

GREENS (HIGH IN NITROGEN)

✳ Grass clippings
✳ Food scraps
✳ Raw vegetables
✳ Raw fruit
✳ Coffee grounds
✳ Tea leaves (loose or bags)
✳ Pet fur or human hair
✳ Herbaceous materials—any trimmings from annual and perennial flowers, vegetable and fruit plants
✳ Animal manures (only if the animals are herbivores)

BROWNS (HIGH IN CARBON)

✳ Dried leaves (you choose to shred or not; they break down faster if shredded)
✳ Straw and hay
✳ Corncobs
✳ Woody materials— twigs, trimmings from hedges, dried stalks (cut into small pieces)
✳ Wood ash
✳ Untreated sawdust
✳ Wood chips (small amounts only; they take a long time to break down)
✳ Newspaper, cardboard, paper towels that have been used to wipe your hands (shred into small pieces and don't put too much in the bin at once)
✳ Eggshells

There are several items you should not add to your home composter: material from diseased plants; feces from carnivorous animals; paper towels soiled with commercial cleaning products; and food wastes such as dairy, meat, and oils.

I choose not to compost plants with weed seeds because I can't be sure that the bins I use at my community garden will get hot enough to destroy those seeds, as we use a cold, passive style of composting. We don't use herbicides at the community garden, but if we did, I wouldn't put the trimmings from plants treated with them into the compost bin. If you live in a large city and have municipal compost, the rules about what you can put in their composters differ from those for the one you have in your backyard. Industrial composters operate at far hotter temperatures and can kill things like pathogens and weed seeds, and you can put pretty much any food scraps (including meat and dairy), as well as wastes such as cat litter, into them.[4] —SN

For best results, follow a few basic rules about what types of wastes to put into your compost bin.

Can I compost rhubarb leaves and the parts of other poisonous plants?

Absolutely! While rhubarb leaves do contain significant concentrations of oxalic acid—hence their being designated as poisonous if ingested by people—they are perfectly fine for the compost heap. The bacterial and fungal microbes that do the composting work are not affected in the slightest and happily decompose them, and, in the process, break down the oxalic acid. You could even have an entire compost pile of rhubarb leaves and the result would be compost that behaves the same way as another mixed-plant debris compost.

Incidentally, we consume oxalic acid on a regular basis through spinach, beets, peanuts, cocoa, and other foods. The body can readily process it so long as you don't go overboard on these foods. Too much oxalic acid on an ongoing basis can lead to trouble, including kidney stones.

By the way, you would need to eat eleven pounds (five kilograms) of rhubarb leaves all at once to achieve a level of oxalic acid to be dangerous for you. Have you ever tried one? I did because I was curious, and I can guarantee that no one would fall in love with them! Best to put them in the compost pile or use them as a mulch.[5]—JM

Rhubarb leaves are completely safe for your compost pile.

What does it mean to have fungally or bacterially dominated compost? Why does it matter?

Did you know certain plants benefit from specific kinds of compost? Some compost is high in nitrogen and dominated by bacteria, while other compost is—you guessed it—carbon and fungally dominated. If you want to create compost that leans toward bacterial domination (sounds like something in a superhero movie!), use plenty of nitrogen-rich wastes (greens). Carbons (browns) are going to be the main feature in fungally dominated compost.

So, which plants prefer which type of compost? Bacterially dominated compost is the best bet for annual vegetables and annual ornamental plants, while fungally dominated compost is suited more toward woody plants such as trees and shrubs and herbaceous perennials. A bacterially dominated compost pile will cook quickly and with a lot of heat, while a fungally dominated compost pile will be slower to break down under cooler temperatures.

Truthfully, your soil—and, in turn, your plants—will take what they can get, so if you can't tailor your compost to your plants, just use whatever you can create. It's all good.[6]—SN

Trees, such as this horse chestnut, will benefit from fungally dominated compost.

The compost I am making smells awful.
How can I fix this?

Compost shouldn't smell yucky, and your neighbours shouldn't complain about the stench wafting from your bin. A fine-tuned compost pile should smell a bit earthy when you turn it, but that's all. If you're noticing a much less desirable odour coming from your composter, you'll need to troubleshoot. Different smells mean different calls to action, so get that sniffer working.

If your compost smells like spoiled food, it *is* probably spoiled food not covered properly with other material, such as dried leaves. Remember, dairy, meat, and oils shouldn't go in the composter. If you accidentally threw some in there, remove them ASAP. Ew.

If your compost smells like sulphur (rotten eggs!), then you're probably looking at an issue of not enough oxygen and too much water. Turn the compost more frequently. Mix in some more brown material, such as dried leaves or straw.

If your compost smells like ammonia (think of glass cleaner), you've got too many nitrogen-based wastes (greens) in there. Loads of fresh grass clippings tend to be frequent contributors to this kind of upset in compost bins. Don't add too many at once—and if you can set them somewhere to dry out in the sun a bit before adding them to your bin, give that a shot. You can also try adding more browns to the bin to offset the overabundance of greens, or simply remove some of the excess greens.[7] —SN

This beautiful, crumbly stuff shouldn't stink.

Help! Ants have taken over my composter. What can I do?

This is more of an annoying problem than a serious one, but it does indicate your compost pile is likely too dry and cool to be top-notch. For the wastes to decompose, they need to be moist (but not soaking wet). Adding water to your compost pile when it is on the dry side will both discourage ants, which hate wet sites, and keep your compost pile humming along as it should. If you are hot composting, add water, then turn the pile, ensuring all parts of it are dampened. (Turning your compost will also keep the ants at bay—they do not like being disturbed—and if their habitat is in upheaval, they will be less likely to make a nest.) For cold composters, just add the water to the top of the pile, and allow it to gradually percolate through. An efficient compost pile will heat up more quickly than a dry, static one, and the heat will also encourage the ants to move on. Generally, if your compost pile is above 140°F (60°C), you probably won't see many ants.[8]—SN

What is leaf mould? What does it do?

Leaf mould is fantastic stuff! Plus, it is free.

Mould is a rotten name for leaf mould, as it implies . . . well . . . mould. Leaf compost is a more appropriate term as that is exactly what you are doing—composting leaves. Unlike with regular composting, you are working with a material almost entirely consisting of carbon. So it takes time for those leaves to break down, but you come away with a super soil conditioner that builds organic matter in the soil, improves water-holding capacity, and builds soil life. What leaf mould doesn't contain is nutrients, so it is not a replacement for regular compost.

The technique is simple and comes with three variations, according to your taste. In the fall, gather as many leaves as you can, from woody, disease-free plants. The first method involves stuffing them into plastic bags, tying off the ends, and then poking a few holes in the sides to allow for airflow. Every so often, toss the bags around and add some water if they look too dry. The second method is the easiest. Pile the leaves into a big pile in a corner of your yard, and let them be, watering them every so often so they stay moist, plus turning to aerate. The third method involves containing them in a bin, preferably mesh or chicken wire for lots of air. You'll also want to monitor the bin for moisture and aeration.

Depending on the weather and how often you attend to the leaves, you will have crumbly leaf compost in six months to a year that you can use to amend your soil or use as mulch on your beds. You can even add it to potting soil to reduce the amount of peat moss needed. Should you want to speed up the process, crumble the leaves ahead of time. I get kids to jump on a pile I have built up. Works a treat! You can also cover your bags, pile, or bin with a tarp, which aids in keeping temperatures consistent, boosts humidity, and conserves moisture.

Making leaf mould is one of my favourite things to do each fall, and I try to have some on hand during the growing season as I prefer to use it as mulch. My only problem is making enough![9]—JM

*This pail of autumn goodness is ready to
be transformed into leaf mould.*

Amendments and
Fertilizers

3

What are the differences between organic, inorganic, synthetic, and natural fertilizers?

Gardening has a lot of terminology. Sometimes it is clear what a term means, and I'll go further—sometimes it can be manipulated to make something seem what it may not be, even to the point of being meaningless.

"Organic" is such a term, loaded with manifold connotations, and never more so than in gardening. Strictly speaking, and from a chemist's point of view, to be organic, a substance needs to contain a carbon atom (C), the sixth element in the periodic table, and will almost always have a carbon-hydrogen (C-H) bond. Inorganic compounds generally do not have this bond. There are many other differences between the two types, but from a gardener's perspective, and according to the learning app website byjus.com, "organic compounds mainly result from the activities of living beings." It then follows that inorganic compounds, also

Plants grown in containers require regular additions of fertilizers to maintain a fabulous appearance!

per byjus.com, are "obtained from the natural processes, which are not related to any of the life forms on Earth or any result of human experiments, which are conducted in laboratories."[1]

That makes it easy for me! Using this guideline:

Organic fertilizers are those derived from life forms of any sort, such as fish or kelp meal.

Inorganic fertilizers are from non-life forms, such as volcanic rock dust or greensand.

Because "organic" is such a loaded term that is easily misconstrued, today you'll find fertilizers characterized as being natural, which can be either organic or inorganic, but are minimally processed. Taking the fish example, you could fish a fish out of a river, bring it home, and bury it in the garden. Or you could take the fish bones and grind them up to the consistency of meal (think cornmeal) and use them, too. Easy to apply, less odour, and no cats digging up the garden but the same great results. Both of these examples would be organic fertilizers.

Likewise, you could bury a rock in your garden and hope in the next aeon it will release its chemicals to benefit the soil, or you can grind it up into the consistency of flour and it will help the garden in a much shorter time. This would be an inorganic but natural fertilizer.

Natural fertilizers require soil life to convert the chemicals into forms that plants can access. As a result, these fertilizers support not only plant life but also soil life and the symbiotic relationships between them. They also contribute to soil improvement as they contain organic matter. Nutrient levels, if specified, can vary and are only approximations, and the fertilizers are converted over time, which reduces the potential for runoff or leaching out of your soil.

Synthetic fertilizers then are literally synthesized by man. They are usually made from petroleum, which is organic in nature, and will have chemical forms present of minerals and nutrients, readily available to plants. They may be from inorganic materials, which have been heavily processed to release their chemicals.

These fertilizers contain specific formulations of nutrients, usually nitrogen, phosphorus, and potassium—for example, 10-10-10. Secondary, micro or trace nutrients may or may not be present.

Synthetic fertilizers have to be applied carefully to avoid toxic buildup in the soil and may readily leach out of the soil as they are water soluble. As the nutrients they provide are already in chemical forms that are available to plants, the symbiotic relationship between soil life and plants will be impacted negatively. However, they do promote rapid growth and are formulated for specific needs. Approximately a third of our petroleum is used as fertilizer around the world, an integral part of the Green Revolution of the 1970s.[2]—JM

These beauties are obviously getting the nutrients they need to flourish.

What do the numbers on a package of fertilizer mean?

The three numbers on a fertilizer bag represent the percentage, by weight, of the primary macronutrients found in the contents: nitrogen, phosphorus, and potassium (listed on the periodic table as N-P-K). Occasionally, you'll see a fourth number, representing sulphur (S). But . . . it's not quite as simple as all that. You'll have to do a little math if you want to make sure you're adding the correct amounts of each nutrient to your soil. Okay, haul out your calculators and memorize the following information:

On your fertilizer bag, nitrogen is expressed as the elemental form. So that's actually the percentage of N in that bag, by weight. But when it comes to phosphorus, it's expressed as P_2O_5 (phosphorus pentoxide). P_2O_5 isn't actually *in* that bag; it's a unit of measurement that is left over from an old practice used by chemists, involving bone meal, fire, and ash. (Sounds interesting!) To calculate the percentage of elemental phosphorus in the bag, by weight, multiply the number on the bag by 0.436. It's a similar thing with potassium. The measurement refers not to elemental potassium but rather the amount of potassium oxide or potash dissolved in water. To obtain the percentage of elemental potassium by weight, multiply the number on the bag by 0.83.

So if your fertilizer bag says "10-52-10" on it, that means the contents contain 10 percent nitrogen, 22 percent phosphorus, and 8 percent potassium, by weight. In a 2.2-pound (1-kilogram) bag, that translates to 0.22 pounds (100 grams) of nitrogen, 0.48 pounds (220 grams) of phosphorus, and 0.17 pounds (80 grams) of potassium.

Nitrogen aids in the production of more chlorophyll and helps with lush, green growth and foliage development. Phosphorus is useful for important things like strong, healthy root systems, blooming, and fruiting. Potassium is a cell builder, and it plays a big role in assisting plants to withstand stresses such as drought and diseases and to tolerate cold. Depending on the types of plants you are growing, what stage of its life cycle a plant is in, and what time of the year it is, fertilizer requirements may change.

Of course, you'll notice that the macronutrient numbers don't add up to 100 percent. So, what's the rest of the stuff in the bag? It can be any number of things: sand, granular limestone, sawdust, or peat moss. These inert ingredients help keep the fertilizer from drying out and clumping and facilitate easy, even application.[3] —SN

Knowing how much and what type of fertilizer to use will help maintain beautiful plants.

When is the best time to amend your soil?

It sounds a bit strange, but the fall is actually the best time to amend your soil in our part of the world. This is especially true if you live in an area where your soil takes a long time to thaw and dry out in spring and warm up enough to work it without damaging soil aggregates and soil life. We also prefer fall, assuming that winter doesn't make an early appearance, because we find it totally satisfying to be closing out the growing season by preparing for the next one.

In the fall, the soil is already dry and, while cooling, is still relatively warm, and the insects and other soil life likely haven't yet settled in for the winter. The amendments you add have time to sink into the soil, and fertilizers can be worked on by the soil life to convert to forms readily available to plants come spring.

Should you delay till spring, you will have to wait until the soil thaws and warms up before commencing the work, which will delay early sowing and planting. Besides, it is often rainier or snowier in April, and who wants to do that work while cold and wet?

To start, remove all the weeds you can find. Then apply the amendments to the soil surface and lightly till them in to a depth of, say, six inches (fifteen centimetres) at the most. If your beds are needing a lot of work to also improve the soil texture, you may want to work the amendments in to a depth of 1 foot (0.3 metres), but as your soil improves over time, reduce that amount of tillage until you are merely scratching in the new amendments. If you are practising the no-till method, pull back the mulch layer, add the amendments needed, and replace the mulch.

If it is an annual edible bed, smooth the soil for a good seed-sowing surface so that it is ready for the spring. Cover with a layer of winter mulch or burlap sacks for soil protection.

Then you can rest easy over the winter, knowing that while you hibernate, those amendments are getting where they belong throughout the soil profile.[4] —JM

What is side-dressing? How do I add it to my garden?

Side-dressing is sort of like adding salad dressing to your salad to make it taste better!

But instead of adding oil and vinegar, you are adding fertilizers to those crops that are either heavy feeders and/or long-maturing plants. Brassicaceae plants, including cabbage, cauliflower, broccoli, Brussels sprouts, and kale, and root crops, such as beets, carrots, and parsnips, all benefit from additional nutrients as they are heavy feeders. Tomatoes, eggplant, corn, and all members of the squash family also welcome the extra fertilizer they are given periodically throughout the season. The ones that don't need side-dressing are quick crops such as radishes and light feeders such as lettuces, unless their colour is too light, and those nitrogen fixers in the legume family. Perennial plants can be side-dressed too, often in a circle away from their crowns.

The technique is simple. About four inches (ten centimetres) from the stems of your growing plants, create a shallow furrow along the rows on either side. If they are big plants such as tomatoes, it is better to create a circle around the plant. Either sprinkle solid fertilizer or dribble liquid fertilizer along the rows or circles and lightly cover with your planting medium. Then water it well so that it has the best chance to get down into the soil profile.

Best choices for fertilizer are either worm compost, fish emulsion, compost extract, or other liquid fertilizers. Be careful to not overdo it. Too much fertilizer, too often, can change the taste of your edibles and may potentially contribute salts to the soil, leading to root damage, and may reduce productivity. Most edible crops and perennials should be side-dressed only once during the season, though those tomatoes might enjoy a second serving.

Then sit back and watch those plants grow![5] —JM

Eggshells in the garden: a good idea or not?

If you glance at any gardening social media pages, you'll see a zillion claims about eggshells and how awesome they are. They supposedly cure blossom-end rot (BER) in tomatoes, slaughter slugs with impunity, add a ton of nutrients to your soil, and make magic with your compost. Some of that is definitely not true, and some of it is only partially true.

Eggshells from chickens and other poultry do contain some nutrients—mostly calcium, but also magnesium, phosphorus, and potassium. Those two thin membranes found just under the eggshell are made of keratin (just like our hair!), and they are, interestingly, a source of organic matter containing proteins that eventually break down into nitrogen once they've been munched on by micro-organisms in the soil.

Eggshells are totally okay for use as a source of nutrients. Just remember they need to be broken down, and with the way they are designed, with that crazy hard shell, they are a bit of a challenge for soil micro-organisms to decompose. And that's even if you crush or pulverize them first! Don't expect a speedy release of any kind of minerals for plants to take up—decomposition can take months or years, which makes them less than ideal even as additives for your compost pile. Also, does your soil even need calcium? I would suspect if you do a soil test, you'll find that yours doesn't. So, while using eggshells in the garden won't do any harm to your plants, they are limited in their value.

As for blossom-end rot, using eggshells to help your tomatoes isn't going to do much. Your soil probably isn't deficient in calcium, unless you are growing in containers and the calcium supply has been exhausted. It's more likely that the calcium in your soil isn't available for use by the plants. Consistent watering will help with that, not adding more calcium. Since eggshells are tricky to decompose, they don't make the calcium they have speedily available for use by plants. By the time the calcium gets to your tomato plants, you've probably already seen the mushy black signs of BER on your fruit.

And about the slugs and snails? If they could laugh, they would be chortling heartily every time they see you've set out a razor-wire line of eggshell fragments for them to cross. Recent studies have shown the sharp edges don't bother them at all.[6]—SN

Are coffee grounds useful in the garden?

Coffee grounds are literally ground-up coffee beans we brew for our get-me-going drink in the morning. It makes no sense to throw them into the landfill. We are talking organic matter, containing a number of nutrients, including nitrogen, potassium, magnesium, calcium, copper, and other trace elements.

The active ingredient in coffee (*Coffea* spp.) is, of course, caffeine, and there is lots of it per cup. Turns out when our mums told us that drinking coffee would stunt our growth, they were right, at least when it applies to plant growth. The jury is out on human growth!

It appears that several species in different plant families, such as coffee, cacao, and tea, independently evolved the ability to synthesize caffeine. This is called convergent evolution, and it is indeed a great adaption for survival.[7] Since caffeine is allelopathic, the caffeine-laden leaves that fall from coffee, tea, and cacao plants make it difficult for other plants around them to grow properly. Hence the stunting. Caffeine also wards off pests, as high enough doses of caffeine are toxic to insects that like coffee, tea, and cacao plants. Low amounts of caffeine are also present in the nectar of these species. Like us, bees and other pollinators enjoy the buzz it gives them!

Which gets us back to whether we should use coffee grounds in our gardens. Coffee grounds still contain relatively high loads of caffeine and, used indiscriminately in our compost, as mulch, or tilled into the soil, could have negative effects on surrounding plants, especially seeds germinating, newly transplanted seedlings, and tomatoes. Likewise, coffee also has antibacterial qualities so may have some adverse effects on soil life, be it microbial on up to earthworms. Given their small size, coffee grounds also compact easily and can create a barrier to water infiltration and aeration.

If you choose to use them as a soil amendment because of their high concentration of organic matter, I recommend that you put your morning coffee grounds in the compost, but don't get big bags of them from your local roaster and dump them in. Coffee grounds may be brown, but they are considered a green for composting purposes, due to their high nitrogen content. Adding too many coffee grounds could throw off the ratio of browns to greens for effective composting.

Sprinkle them thinly over soil or till the grounds into your soil lightly but not where seeds and seedlings are. Your perennial beds are calling. However, if you have a really weed-infested bed, maybe they have a place suppressing growth!

Don't bother using coffee grounds to acidify your high-pH soil. They are only mildly acidic. You would need an awful lot to make a difference, and it would kill a lot of things from plants to microbes along the way. They aren't very good for slug or ant control either. If you have motivated slugs or ants, they will cross them anyway to get to the good stuff.[8] —JM

It's a good idea to let fresh manure age in the compost pile before using it in your garden.

I just obtained a load of fresh manure from a farmer. How long do I have to let it mature before I can use it in my garden?

Animal feces (particularly from livestock such as cattle, horses, sheep, and chickens) are often used as an organic amendment for agricultural and garden soils, to provide nutrients and boost poor structure. It's good practice not to use fresh manure straight from the (ahem) source. It usually contains too much nitrogen, which may burn crops, and, besides, the odour is pretty offensive. Composting manure also decreases the risk of pathogens such as E. *coli*, salmonella, and giardia entering the food system. Park the manure in a pile, and let it sit and decompose for approximately two years—the longer the better.

Another issue with many types of animal manure is that it can potentially introduce weed seeds into your soil. The weeds may have been in the animal's bedding or litter that then gets mixed with fresh manure, or the seeds may have been deposited by the animals producing the manure. Some weed seeds may be sterilized when the manure is composted, but many will not be.

If you have a bin-style composter, you can throw the manure in there and let it do its thing over time. Creating a pile in an unused area of your yard will also work, although it is considerably less attractive. (Bear in mind that if there is grass underneath the pile, it will die.)

If you notice it getting too dry, add some water to dampen, not soak, the pile. There is no need to break out the garden hose if you get regular rainfall in your area.

You can accelerate the process by heating the composting pile. It will require a balance of carbon and nitrogen as well as oxygen and moisture. If the pile is too wet, it will need additions of dried leaves. (If the manure contains bedding such as straw, there will be little or no need for extra carbon.) The ratio you're seeking is about fifteen parts of carbon (leaves or bedding) to one part nitrogen (manure). The pile must be turned at least three times a week. Finally, the temperature of the pile must reach a minimum of 140°F (60°C). Keep a compost thermometer handy! If you are diligent with supplying the correct ratio of C:N and sufficient aeration, you'll have composted manure in four to six weeks. As with any hot composting process, watch the pile carefully as it cooks, as there is a risk—slight, but still possible—that it may combust.

Do *not*, I repeat, do *not* compost the wastes of carnivorous animals, such as cats and dogs, in your home composter. It doesn't matter how good your composter is, it will never, ever reach the temperatures needed to kill pathogens that may be in Fido or Fluffy's feces.

The key thing to remember about the content of manure is that, just like with compost, ingredients may vary. The nutrients in a sample of manure will vary from animal to animal. Factors such as the animal's age, what it ate, and even what type of bedding it used will all make a difference.

Animals such as cattle and sheep are ruminants and have extremely efficient digestive systems. Sheep have potassium-rich manure. Cattle manure is not considered a top source of macronutrients, but it is quite balanced, with slightly higher nitrogen levels. When I worked in a garden centre, I was often asked about the difference between cattle and steer manure, as we carried both types. Cattle manure primarily refers to the leavings of dairy cows (and occasionally from cattle raised for beef), which tend to have a diet heavy in forage crops, such as alfalfa. Steers are often raised on more grain-based diets than dairy cattle, which may result in manure higher in nitrogen and salts than that of their dairy counterparts.

The manure of poultry, such as turkeys and chickens, is very high in nitrogen, as it is a combination of feces and urine. Compost this stuff well or you'll end up with problems. On the bright side, weed seeds are usually not an issue associated with manure from poultry.

Horse manure is often combined with urine and bedding, and it is a rich source of nitrogen, even higher than cattle manure. Horses don't digest their food as thoroughly as cattle do, so horse manure is often riddled with weed seeds.

Rabbit manure is also typically mixed with urine. It is a good source of nitrogen, and it is usually free from weed seeds. Some gardeners claim it is safe to use fresh from the bunny, but I would recommend composting it first just to be on the safe side.[9] —SN

Everyone seems to be using Epsom salt in their gardens. Should I amend my soil with it?

Ah, Epsom salt. According to millions of gardeners on the internet, these coarse granules of magnesium sulphate may be successfully employed in the garden as, variously, an insecticide, a fungicide, an herbicide, and a fertilizer, among countless other things. While I will neither argue against nor validate these claims, I can state that, unfortunately, according to peer-reviewed scientific research, magnesium sulphate is actually not ideal for treating the one thing it is most often used for: combatting a deficiency of the micronutrients magnesium and sulphur in the soil. Sure, it works, but there are better ways than Epsom salt to deliver magnesium or sulphur to plants—ways that are easier for the plants to take up by their roots. Compost is the very best solution (bet you knew I'd say that!).

If you've done a soil test to make sure your soil is actually deficient in magnesium and sulphur and requires an addition, consider treating it with elemental sulphur, available in a powdered form from garden centres. Problematic magnesium deficiencies can be treated with calcium magnesium carbonate, also known as dolomitic lime—which you definitely don't want to go overboard with. If your soil isn't deficient—and most prairie soils are not—Epsom salt is not required. If your soil test comes up with a magnesium deficiency, it could be that you have too much phosphorus in the soil. It sounds ridiculous, but soil chemistry is complicated: excessive phosphorus will prevent plants from taking up magnesium, in which case, adding Epsom salt is not going to work.

If you want to use Epsom salt, I'm not going to say you can't or shouldn't. It is cheap, plentiful, and easy to apply. It won't hurt your plants unless you add too much. And some gardeners really swear by it. Personally, my favourite—and recommended—way to use Epsom salt is to lower my creaky old bones into a steaming bath filled with it, après gardening.[10]—SN

Roses will bloom nicely without amendments of banana peels.

What about that throwing-a-banana-peel-in-the-soil-near-your-rose-bushes thing?

The thing about banana peels is they contain potassium and magnesium, both of which are necessary for all flower-producing plants, not just roses. The peels also break down quickly.

However, adding banana peels around your rose bushes is not likely to provide all that they need to be healthy and to produce gorgeous blooms. Not only that, but the peels may attract mice and other animals to enjoy the snack.

Some gardeners will dry them inside, chop them up finely, and sprinkle them around, so they break down even faster. Others will bury the peels in the soil around the plants or place them at the bottom of planting holes. In essence, that is a form of pit composting, where one buries composting materials in a hole and lets them compost in situ. The danger of doing this underneath or beside a new or established plant is nitrogen inhibition, when all the soil life breaking down the peels uses up available nitrogen, and once it gets in short supply in the soil, the plant suffers.

Mind you; you would have to eat and bury a lot of banana peels to get either the positive benefit or the negative effect.

Me, I just chuck them in the compost bin, after removing the pesky stickers. Not that I haven't been known to eat a banana in the garden and discard the skin conveniently beside said rose bush every so often.[11] —JM

I have read that peat moss isn't an easily renewable resource. Should I use coir instead?

The use of both peat moss and coir fibre is a minefield of ethical and sustainable environmental issues and (mis)information. They both have pros and cons.

First, let's look at what each of these natural amendments is and how it is produced.

Also known as peat moss or sphagnum peat moss, peat is primarily found in northern temperate zones, where there are cool temperatures and ample precipitation. Peat grows in bogs in wetland areas where plant debris, such as mosses, sedges, and shrubby plants, due to anaerobic and acidic conditions, is not able to fully decompose. All this takes time, and many of the world's peat bogs were formed after the end of the last ice age, some 12,000 years ago. They are not static as peat continues to accumulate slowly at a rate of a millimetre or so a year in the wild. Canada has approximately 25 percent of the world's peat bogs, some 294 million acres (119 million hectares), of which approximately 0.02 percent are currently being harvested under fairly strict and sustainable practices set out by the Canadian Sphagnum Peat Moss Association.[12] Doing the math, the Earth is accumulating peat faster than it is being removed, at least in Canada.

Once harvested, peat is dried. The traditional method was just leaving it out in the open so the water would evaporate. In modern harvesting, the water is extracted and the material is compressed. There are different grades of peat, depending on the plant material that comprises it and how it is processed. Not all peat is sphagnum peat moss, which is the best quality.

Coir fibre (coco coir or just coir) is the fibre found inside coconut husks. It is primarily the debris from the coconut industry, mostly from South and Southeast Asia. The coconuts we see in our stores have had their leathery skins removed along with a lot of the fibre between the skins and the inner husks or seeds. Some of that fibre is used to make fishing nets, rope, mats, and other household objects, but much of it is a waste product.

Coir requires a fair amount of processing to make it usable as a garden amendment. Depending on the maturity of the coconuts, high levels of sodium are removed through washing with a brine, sea water, or fresh water in a process called rhetting.[13] This process may cause significant water pollution as an array of organic substances are released into waterways. Once processed, coir is dehydrated and compressed into bales for transport. Additionally, questions have been raised about the health and working conditions of those involved in coir processing in the coir pith factories.[14] Also, once coir is shipped overseas and is no longer available as a soil amendment for the groves that produced the coconuts, farmers need to source other organic matter to replenish their soils. Both require transportation to our gardens, though peat, being a Canadian source, has much less of a carbon footprint than coir.

Both peat and coir are amendments with little in the way of nutrients to contribute to the soil. Their value lies in the amount of moisture they absorb and slowly release into the soil, along with their fibrous biomass contributing to the soil's organic matter to improve soil aggregation.

Peat will absorb ten to twenty times its weight in water, and coir will absorb eight to nine times its weight in moisture. Peat is rather acidic (depending on its composition, it is in the range of 3.5 to 4 pH) and, after factoring in one's individual soil, may need to be amended with lime to increase its pH to neutral. Coir is naturally in the range of 5.2 to 6.8 pH.[15] Coir has significant amounts of lignin and cellulose and resists degrading in the soil for a long time. If using it to grow seedlings, it can be washed and reused many times. Peat, being of less durable materials, breaks down fairly quickly. Both peat and coir require rehydration before use, with peat being hydrophobic at first. Take the time to thoroughly wet each, ensuring they are sufficiently damp, before using in the garden.

Do we use peat or coir in our gardens? As a rule, no, not as a regular garden soil amendment, as both have significant impacts in terms of environmental sustainability, especially if sustainability is partly defined as "Do no harm." Compost does the same work and can be made right in the garden. We will use peat if we are remediating compacted, degraded soil highly deficient in organic matter. We also use peat in growing mediums for seedlings and in container growing mediums.

But, in the end, the choice is up to each gardener whether to use either or neither. —JM

Should I use sand in my garden to improve soil drainage? If so, what kind of sand should I purchase?

Considering that sandy soils have far better drainage than those with a high clay content, it seems to make sense that adding sand to clay soils would be an inexpensive and easy fix. Not so!

Not all sand is created equal. Most of it will actually give your soil the texture of cement if you combine it with clay and then add water. Fixing that problem will take years! If you think sand is the answer, a bit won't hurt, but make sure you purchase horticultural sand, available at garden centres. Don't get play sand, as you'll regret it. And, yes, horticultural sand is expensive.

What your clay soil really needs is a lot more organic matter to improve the structure and, therefore, the drainage. Compost and leaf mould are good additions to make instead of sand, and they're cheaper because you can build them yourself.

Some gardeners like to mix in a bit of horticultural sand to their growing medium recipes for their containers, and it works nicely, particularly if you are growing succulents. You can also substitute grit that is sold for use with pet birds. —SN

If you wish to use sand in your garden, choose horticultural sand like this, as it is very gritty.

Should I use wood ash in my garden? Why or why not?

It always seems a shame to not upcycle wood ash from our fireplaces or wood stoves, but whether to use it in your garden comes down to: it depends.

Wood ash typically contains 30 to 40 percent calcium carbonate, which, by the way, is an ingredient in garden lime. To a greater or lesser degree, it also contains potassium, phosphorus, magnesium, aluminum, sodium, and not a few trace elements. It may also include heavy metals such as lead and cadmium as well as chemicals from wood preservatives, depending on the source.

The big concern with using wood ash is that it will increase pH. Most prairie soils are already on the alkaline side of life, and wood ash will serve to increase that alkalinity over time if used consistently. The potential for heavy metal contamination makes it undesirable around the vegetable garden, too. It is also difficult to ascertain the quantities of minerals since there will be varying levels, depending on the type of wood and where it was grown.

Wood ash can also be toxic to soil in the compost heap or garden given the potential levels of specific elements, with no more than 1 pound (0.45 kilograms) per 100 square feet (9.3 square metres) of soil recommended.

All in all, I steer away from wood ash. It isn't worth the real and potential downsides, and there are many other fertilizers we can use for calcium, potassium, and phosphorus deficiencies in our soil that do not come with the risks.

As Steve Solomon and Erica Reinheimer put it in their book, *The Intelligent Gardener*, "the best place for a wildcard like wood ashes is back into the forest from whence they originated (and to save the trees from shock, spread it thinly)."[16]

Tip: Wood ash can be useful as slug control if used sparingly. They are repelled by it, so it might be a good choice, if carefully sprinkled around your hostas. —JM

What are the best amendments to "lighten" heavy clay soil?

If you've been reading this book from front to back, you're totally going to know what I'm about to recommend here: compost, compost, and more compost. Chuck in some leaf mould, too. The key is to boost the organic matter in your soil, which will help improve soil structure. Amendments such as perlite, peat moss, and sheep wool pellets can also be used to increase porosity and aeration in soil.

Gypsum, otherwise known as calcium sulphate, is also widely touted as a "clay-breaker." It is primarily used as an amendment on highly compacted, heavy clay soils. While use of gypsum will result in better percolation of water, help with drainage, and reduce the crusting of topsoil, it is not a gardener's best option for these tasks. It is an expensive product to purchase and large amounts must be used to have any effect; as well, the good work it does actually only lasts for a few months, at best. Repeat applications every year (and sometimes more than once per growing season) are necessary. It does not offer any sort of soil fertility, cannot alter soil pH, and poses only a short-term solution to soil structure issues. It can also introduce way too much calcium into soils that do not require it, so if you decide to use it, be sure to do a soil test to determine if calcium is even required. There is also some evidence that it can interfere with the beneficial relationship between mycorrhizal fungi and the roots of some plants, which may be another deterrent.

Besides being an excellent source of calcium sulphate, gypsum is extremely useful to remove sodium from affected soils (a frequent problem in large-scale agriculture). If these are issues that require rectifying in your garden, gypsum may be the answer. But for most prairie gardeners, it's an unnecessary cost.[17]

Unfortunately, there isn't an instant fix to lighten our clay-based prairie soil, but if you've been gardening for a few years, you already know no such thing exists. You have to keep plugging away, and that's part of the fun of it. Keep adding organic matter regularly, every year, and give all the soil micro-organisms time to work with it. I highly recommend the use of compost—and compost combined with the planting of cover crops is even better.

If you are absolutely fed up with your field soil and don't want to keep amending, try gardening above ground in containers and raised beds, where you can better manage the condition of the soil. —SN

Gardening in a raised bed can be an excellent option if your garden soil is simply too heavy and compacted to use.

I would like to amend my soil to help with conserving water. What are the pros and cons of soil amendments that help with drainage and retaining water?

Gardeners who are looking for amendments that help retain water and assist with drainage have many options to choose from. Those puffy white Styrofoam-looking kernels commonly found in potting soil mixes are called perlite (SiO_2). Perlite is formed from a type of volcanic glass containing water vapour, which is trapped by cooled lava. The glass is mined, then heated to 1,560 to 1,650°F (850 to 900°C). The water molecules expand and "pop" the minerals in the glass.

Perlite is non-combustible, so it is often used in construction, for ceiling tiles, roof, and pipe insulation. Horticultural-grade perlite works very well in gardening applications because it is porous and its sterility helps prevent common seedling issues such as damping off. Excellent water retention and drainage make perlite a popular growing medium in hydroponic and non-hydroponic systems alike. The large air-filled pockets between the kernels promote optimum root development and allow water and nutrients to move freely. When mixed with soil, perlite helps to reduce compaction.

Although perlite is inexpensive and easy to obtain, alas, it is a non-renewable resource. It cannot be replenished in the site it is mined from (presumably unless there is more volcanic activity at the source). Fortunately, a small amount of glass will produce a lot of perlite. It may be washed and dried and can be reused many times.

Ensure proper safety equipment is worn while handling perlite: a dust mask and gloves are essential, as breathing in the dust can be harmful. Moistening perlite with water before using it can help keep the dust down.[18]

Vermiculite can also be used to amend soil and aid in water retention. It is a naturally occurring composite of hydrated silicates of aluminum, iron, and magnesium. When processed with extreme heat, the unique molecular structure of vermiculite causes it to expand and "exfoliate" into laminated sheets. After it is broken into pieces, chunks of vermiculite resemble the rock mica. It is mined all over the world, with the United States, China, South Africa, and Brazil being top producers. Vermiculite is highly fire-resistant, which is why it is primarily used in insulation in homes and businesses.

Vermiculite has huge benefits: it cannot rot, mould, or readily decompose. Like perlite, it is completely sterile, so it does not promote disease. Lightweight and porous, it is touted to be even better than perlite at retaining water. This makes it very useful as a growing medium for plants requiring high moisture. Vermiculite can also help to improve aeration in soil, which helps with root development.

Proponents of Mel Bartholomew's square-foot-gardening technique (see our book *The Prairie Gardener's Go-To for Small Spaces* for an in-depth explanation of this gardening method) use a great deal of vermiculite in their soil mixes: the recommended blend is ⅓ coarse-grade vermiculite to ⅓ peat moss to ⅓ compost. This mix promotes good drainage and aeration and helps to reduce soil compaction.

There is more than one grade of vermiculite: the coarse (particles larger than ½ inch or 1.27 centimetres in diameter) is the one square-foot gardeners use, while the fine grade (particles of approximately ⅒ inch or 0.25 centimetres in diameter) are most often used for seeding trays. Medium (³⁄₁₀ inch or 0.76 centimetres) or large-grade particles are often found in store-bought potting mixes, and these sizes are also excellent for storing those tender bulbs lifted out from the soil during the winter months. Vermiculite can be crushed during transportation and storage, and coarse grade can be transformed into dust if not handled carefully.

Be sure to wear gloves when handling vermiculite. You may see references online to asbestos and vermiculite; this is not a concern with horticultural vermiculite or even with today's vermiculite used for insulation. In the 1970s and 1980s, a vermiculite mine in Libby, Montana, produced a large amount of vermiculite that was contaminated with asbestos. This was sold all over North America as construction insulation. Unfortunately, some of the mine workers became ill, and subsequently the use of the material from that mine was discontinued. It has not been sold in Canada for decades.[19]

Zeolite is also worth considering as an amendment to improve water retention. Zeolite minerals are volcanic in origin and contain upwards of fifty elements.

Depending on the source, zeolite includes micronutrients or trace elements, but mainly silicon, aluminum, and oxygen. What is unique about the mineral is the channels and cavities in each tiny piece that act to absorb up to 60 percent of its weight in water, as well as water-soluble nutrients such as nitrogen that readily leach out of the soil.[20] Even better, the tiny shards work to build good soil texture, reduce compaction, and improve aeration and drainage in clay-based soils. It also works to buffer the pH in soils. Long lasting, it does not break down in the soil like other amendments through soil microbial action.[21]

We usually apply zeolite to perennial beds every other year or so, by sprinkling it on the surface and scratching it in. Eventually, it makes its way down into the soil profile to do its work. If renovating a bed or creating a new raised or in-ground bed, add it to the soil mix, roughly 1 pound (0.45 kilograms) to 1 square yard (0.8 square metre) of soil. It can also be added into potting soil, just a handful per container. You can even sprinkle it on an existing lawn and rake it in to improve the soil beneath the turf.[22]

Finally, we think that sheep wool pellets have much to recommend them. Made from wool sheared from the belly and the back end (ahem) of sheep—better known as the woolly parts that aren't typically trimmed for use in textiles—it is then pelletized and sold to gardeners to help reduce watering frequency for plants growing in containers. Forget those hydrogel crystals—wool pellets are safe for use with edible and ornamental crops alike. The wool holds water and slowly releases it over time, meaning you don't have to haul out the watering can quite so often. The pellets can also help with soil aeration, increasing the pore spaces between soil particles, and giving your plant's roots a place to spread out.

These little balls of fuzz can help reduce watering frequency in your container garden.

Wool pellets also are a source of nitrogen, as well as calcium, magnesium, iron, and sulphur. The nutrients are not immediately available to plants, but are slowly released over several months. Use approximately ½ cup (64 grams) of wool pellets per 1-gallon (3.78-litre) container.

The jury is still out on another purported use of wool pellets: Will they stop slugs and snails from going on a slow rampage through your garden? According to proponents, the tiny barbs found in wool fibres—the very reason some of us itch so much when we wear wool—may also be annoying to these soft-bodied molluscs. But, as the use of eggshells and other sharp surfaces to deter slugs and snails has been widely debunked, it seems likely the wool won't bug the slimy creatures like it does us.[23] — SN & JM

Will using volcanic rock dust in my garden make my produce healthier and increase yields?

Volcanic basalt rock dust has been used as a natural amendment in agriculture and horticulture since the 1930s. The premise is that land around active volcanoes is known to be extremely fertile, once the volcano has simmered down again!

The reason for the fertility is the large amounts of volcanic material deposits in the soils. While this material does not contain any macronutrients plants need, it includes a fair number of minerals and trace elements necessary for plant health.

Volcanic rock dust is literally volcanic rock that has been finely ground to the consistency of flour. The idea is that small particles are more easily broken down in the soil and can release their chemicals to be further degraded by soil life and converted to plant-available forms.

There is a fair amount of opinion on both sides of the fence as to whether rock dust does anything for the soil at all or is the boon that companies marketing it claim it to be. If rock dust doesn't contribute to our soil fertility, then it is a waste of money and resources. However, there is some science-based research indicating benefits as well as a long history of use around the world.[24]

If it does work, the benefits are increased plant health and vigour, along with more bountiful harvests in terms of size, taste, and texture. Plus, there is a side benefit of plants having better natural defences against pests and diseases.

The premise is that our soils need these minerals, and the process of adding rock dust is remineralization. In our instant world, what is not specified is the amount of time that this process may take before the minerals are in a form to be used as nutrients by plants. Rock takes time to weather, break down, and release its minerals. Grinding it into dust just makes the rock really, really small.

What I can say is that I have consistently used volcanic rock dust in some of my gardens and community gardens for at least five years, and I have seen results. Plants do seem healthier with fewer problems. I have also seen fantastic produce—seeing is believing. Was the produce that good because of the rock dust or because of other factors? Hard to tell, but if you are looking to improve your soil fertility over the long term and for the long haul, it seems to be worth it.[25]—JM

Radishes and other veggies may benefit from soil amended with volcanic rock dust.

Worm castings are an excellent addition to keep
containers looking dazzling all summer long.

Talk to me about the differences between the various animal-based fertilizers and amendments. Should I add them to my soil?

There are many animal-based organic fertilizers to choose from. First, let's talk about bone meal, which has been a traditional, natural fertilizer through the ages. As its name makes clear, it is made from the bones of animals. Unfortunately, its popularity as a standard go-to amendment relied on the traditional method of obtaining it, which was to literally grind up bones, marrow and all, which made it a good all-around fertilizer with nitrogen, phosphorus, calcium, and a number of other minerals. The modern method is to remove the marrow and then steam or bake the bones and grind them down, leaving the insoluble phosphorus and calcium.

Both of these elements are generally present in goodly amounts in our prairie garden soils. These elements also take a long time to be converted by soil life into chemical forms plants can take up. Indiscriminate use, such as the old adage to put bone meal in a hole when planting bulbs to stimulate root growth, can result in a buildup of phosphorus and may detrimentally affect the mycorrhizal fungi relationship with the plants in question.[26] Not only that, while phosphorus is necessary for good root development, it is not a root stimulant. Your bulbs or new plants may even be more prone to be dug up as dogs and other mammals can smell the scent of the bones, which we cannot discern!

The kicker is that in soils with a pH of 7.0 or higher (like ours), the phosphorus in bone meal is largely inert. Acidic soils can convert the phosphorus more readily, and it is appropriate to use bone meal for those soils.

So, if you have a bag, use it up in peat-based potting soil mixes, or toss it into the compost pile. If after a soil test you discover your soil is deficient in phosphorus, there are other, more efficient sources if you need to add this element to your garden.[27]

Blood meal is just as advertised: the dried blood from cattle or hogs that have been harvested for meat. It is an excellent source of nitrogen readily available for use by plants. Granules can be added to your garden soil: about 1 to 1.5 pounds

(450 to 680 grams) is enough for 100 square feet (9.3 square metres). Blood meal is also water soluble, so you can combine it with water before using it. In large quantities, blood meal may be used as a soil acidifier, but that's not the most efficient use for it, and if you are using it in this way, you risk adding too much nitrogen to your soil, which could create a whole new bunch of problems.[28]

When chickens, ducks, and turkeys are harvested for meat, one of the by-products is their feathers, which can be heat processed and ground up into a rich source of nitrogen, creating feather meal. If you want lush, green growth, this is the amendment for you. Feather meal is also sometimes used as a compost accelerator.

One thing about feather meal: it is not water soluble and makes a lousy top-dressing. Mix it in when you are adding other amendments, such as compost, or throw in a few handfuls when you are making your own blends for containers or raised beds. Use 1 pound (0.45 kilograms) per 100 square feet (9.3 square metres) in your in-ground beds. For containers, 1 tablespoon (15 millilitres) of feather meal in a 1-gallon (3.78-litre) pot is enough. There is usually no need to apply feather meal more than once per season. The best time to use it is in the spring.[29]

Finally, you may want to consider worm castings for your garden, which is basically earthworm waste after they have munched down on a meal of soil and organic matter. The castings look a lot like dark, rich compost, and they are full of bacteria, enzymes, partially digested plant matter, and soil. All the microbes in the castings will keep working to decompose the castings further. Worm castings are a good source of nitrogen and calcium, and they are rich in phosphorus. While a little extra nitrogen is usually welcome, if your garden soil is already high in phosphorus, go easy on the worm castings, as overdosing your plants is harmful. Worm castings should be used sparingly.

The terms "vermicompost" and "worm castings" are often used interchangeably, but many gardeners consider vermicompost to be a mixture of worm castings, organic material, shredded and decomposing bedding, eggs, and the worms themselves in an enclosed vermicomposting system. (See also pages 29–30 for more about how worm castings can improve your soil.)[30] —JM & SN

How effective is alfalfa meal as a soil amendment and a fertilizer?

Alfalfa meal is made from dried, ground alfalfa plants. If you've seen alfalfa pellets sold in garden centres or feed stores, that's a compressed form of alfalfa meal. You can rehydrate the pellets by steeping them in a bucket of water, then crumble them up before using them. (Check the ingredients list on the pellet bag before purchasing, however, as some are mixed with binding agents that you don't need in your garden. Get 100 percent alfalfa and you're good to go.)

Alfalfa meal is a good source of nitrogen and, at a secondary level, of phosphorus. It also contains a naturally occurring plant-growth hormone called triacontanol, which is frequently used in commercial agricultural crops to boost productivity and size. One of its claims to fame is it can increase the amount of chlorophyll in plant leaves, which makes them more efficient at photosynthesis. Of course, you're not likely to notice a huge difference in your garden plants if you use alfalfa pellets, but it can't hurt, right?

Alfalfa meal can help improve soil structure over multiple applications—simply mix it together with compost and top-dress your garden beds each year in the spring. A recommended rate of application is 6 pounds (2.7 kilograms) per 100 square feet (9.3 square metres) in your garden bed, or 6 tablespoons (88 millilitres) per each 1-gallon (3.78-litre) container. Alfalfa meal is sometimes used as a nitrogen-based accelerator for stagnant compost piles. If your compost isn't cooking as quickly as you would like it to, first add some water, then throw a couple of handfuls of alfalfa meal into the bins to kick-start the microbial activity.[31]—**SN**

What are my choices if I want to add fish-based fertilizer to my soil?

Fish-based fertilizers include fish emulsion, fish hydrolysate, and fish meal. They are all by-products of the fish processing industries, which means any parts of the fish can be used in the mix, including excrement. Fish meal is dried and ground, while emulsion and hydrolysate are either heat or cold processed and sold as liquids. Depending on the liquid product you purchase, you may need to dilute it with water before applying. Follow the recommended measurements on the package. Fish fertilizers are generally used for the nitrogen they offer plants, but they also contain a broad selection of other macro- and micronutrients. They also contain a large quantity of proteins and oils, which plants can't really use until microbes in the soil have properly digested them.[32]

Another product, shrimp compost (or shrimp manure as it is sometimes sold in stores), is made up of the dried and ground shells and soft tissues of shrimp, which is then mixed with compost or the manure of cattle or sheep. You can also find dried, ground shrimp meal sold without the accompanying compost or manure. While it can be tricky to find on the landlocked prairies, you may be able to order it online.

Shrimp meal contains chitin, a source of nitrogen. It also includes several micronutrients such as calcium, magnesium, and sulphur. It takes a long time for the chitin to break down into a form plants can use, which is why shrimp meal is often mixed with compost or manure—the other ingredients will become available to plants more quickly. As with other amendments, shrimp meal will help improve soil structure as it is consumed by soil micro-organisms.

Other crustaceans and some molluscs may be used as soil amendments as well; examples include crabs, lobsters, crayfish, oysters, mussels, and clams.[33] —SN

Everyone is talking about seaweed fertilizer. Does it really work?

Seaweed-based fertilizer, otherwise known as kelp meal, has one simple ingredient: dried seaweed. It doesn't have a huge concentration of macronutrients (nitrogen, phosphorus, or potassium), but it does contain quite a few micronutrients such as calcium, magnesium, manganese, iron, zinc, and sulphur. It also contains cytokine, a plant growth regulator. Cytokine boosts cell division in root and shoot meristems, and it also improves the development of plants' vascular systems.

If you're adding kelp meal to your container potting medium mix, use about 1 tablespoon (15 millilitres) for a 1-gallon (3.78-litre) pot. In a garden bed, 1 pound (0.45 kilograms) of kelp meal per 100 square feet (9.3 square metres) is all you need. A single top-dressing each year, in the spring, is sufficient.

You can also purchase kelp meal in a concentrated powdered form or even as a tea. If you're using it as a tea, you can apply it more frequently during the growing season, about once per month. Follow the measurements on the package.[34]

Another interesting sea-based soil amendment worth mentioning is called greensand. It is a mineral powerhouse composed of potash, silica, iron oxide, magnesium, lime, and phosphoric acid, as well as approximately thirty other trace minerals. Greensand is a type of gritty glauconite deposit left over from marine beds formed during the Eocene, Cambrian, and Cretaceous periods. It is a limited resource and non-renewable—in fact, the only place it is actively mined today is in North America, in New Jersey. It is also found in small deposits all over the world, including in Britain, France, and areas near the North Sea and the Baltic Sea. The potash it contains helps strengthen plants against disease and stresses. Not only is it useful as a fertilizer, but greensand is often added to clay soils or compacted soils to improve their structure. (Don't expect an instant cure-all, though. You need to apply it year after year and undertake the appropriate cultivation practices to boost soil structure. Check out how to troubleshoot compacted soil on page 106.)

Greensand is not water soluble, so it is best to mix it into your growing medium recipes for containers or raised beds, or to very lightly rake it into in-ground beds. (Remember, we prefer no-till methods and recommend not digging in soil amendments.) In your garden beds, 3 pounds (1.36 kilograms) of greensand per 100 square feet (9.3 square metres) is an advisable rate of application. In a 1-gallon (3.78-litre) container, 2 tablespoons (30 millilitres) of greensand is sufficient.[35] —SN

Kelp meal is chock full of micronutrients.

What is mushroom compost? Is it good for my garden?

Mushroom compost is a bit of a confusing term. It's not actually compost made from mushrooms but rather is the substrate specifically created for mushrooms to grow in. Once the mushrooms have been harvested, the growing medium is not nutritious enough for another batch, so it is (usually, but not always) sterilized and then packaged for home gardeners to use.

Mushroom growers start with a base of straw and chicken or horse manure. Other ingredients may be added: peat moss, animal bedding, potash, gypsum, lime, and ammonium nitrate. Mushroom growers tailor the compost mix for optimum production of the mushroom species they are cultivating. It is cooked at temperatures of over 160°F (70°C) for several weeks. The cured compost is then inoculated with mushroom spawn and pressed into service as a substrate.

After the mushrooms have been harvested, and by the time it gets to the gardener, the substrate is depleted from the mushrooms, so it is not the very best source of nutrients for your garden soil. Use it in conjunction with other amendments and don't rely solely on it. You can also dump it in your compost bins, to mix and mingle with all the organic matter and microbes that you've got in there.

Mushroom compost also tends to have a high salt content, so although you might be tempted to increase the amount you throw in your containers and beds because it's not very rich, don't do it. Definitely don't use mushroom compost with your seedlings; fertilizer burn may result. Focus on mushroom compost's value as a soil conditioner instead of on its nutritional content. Quite often mushroom growers give it away for free, and, as any gardener knows, that's too good of an offer to pass up.[36] —SN

The substrate that these oyster mushrooms are grown on can be reused by gardeners.

What is an effective amendment to increase soil pH?

Dolomite lime (calcium magnesium carbonate) is ground limestone containing magnesium and calcium. It is primarily used to increase the pH of soil (if necessary), and, in turn, maximizes the ability of plants to take up nutrients. The field soil in prairie gardens is likely on the alkaline side, not acidic. Do a soil test before deciding that lime is an option for you—chances are, you don't need it. If your test results indicate the pH does need to be adjusted but you don't need the magnesium that dolomite lime offers, you can use calcitic lime instead (calcium carbonate). Applying lime without testing may lead to imbalances in your soil's chemistry, which can result in more compaction, more weeds, more issues with plant stress, more work for you. If your soil test determines that you need lime, follow the rate of application to a T![37]—**SN**

Mulching and Other Cultural Practices

4

How can soil compaction be reduced?

Let me count the ways!

Don't work or walk on soils that are too cold or too wet. I know it's incredibly difficult to wait in the spring for the soil to completely thaw, but it's really so much better for your soil if you do. The fungi and bacteria found in soils are affected by factors such as cultivation, soil moisture, and soil temperature. Most bacteria are fairly resilient and adaptable—and there are far more of them in soil than fungi—but fungi take a lot longer to develop and don't enjoy being disturbed.

These seedlings are struggling in compacted clay soil.

Create pathways through your garden that don't involve you stepping into the beds. Use stepping stones, mulch, grow turfgrass—whatever you want to do to prevent treading on your valuable soil. Encourage children and pets to use the paths you've created so they don't wear down the soil in your garden either.

Make your garden accessible so you don't have to walk all over it—use raised beds, or make your in-ground beds narrow enough to easily reach across them while you are working.

Avoid adding most types of sand to your garden beds in the hopes that it will improve drainage. (See page 84 for more about why sand is not a cure-all for this problem.)

Use mulch to reduce compaction from heavy rains that have beaten down onto the soil. (This isn't a consistent problem on the prairies, but during the summer we sometimes have storms with significant hard rainfall.)

Add organic matter. You'll notice a theme here, but I can't stress this enough. Planting a cover crop is an excellent idea, as well.[1] —SN

Is it a good idea to till your garden?

When you till a garden, the bed is ploughed and the soil is loosened with the idea that oxygen and water can better reach the root systems of plants. (Tilling also makes it easy to plant—there is a clean slate to work with!) While tilling was also traditionally thought to be a good way to control weeds, we've recently learned it can sometimes do the exact opposite by bringing dormant weed seeds to the surface of the soil, where, given exposure to sunlight, they germinate. Furthermore, tilling may, over time, compromise soil structure and increase the risk of soil erosion from forces such as wind and water.

In no-till gardening, crop residues are left on the soil. Because you do not have to plough, no-till gardening is not as labour intensive or harmful to soil structure as tilling, and there are several benefits to allowing crop residues to decompose on site. The soil will have better water retention and little evaporation will occur. (This means you won't have to water as often!) If you use pesticides and fertilizers, there will be less of a chance they will run off into nearby lakes and rivers, as they will be impeded by the leftover plant matter. As well, planted soil contains and attracts many more living organisms than bare soil—and much of that life is in a good position to help your crops grow and thrive.

One huge drawback to no-till gardening is that seeding or transplanting is done by digging planting holes through the residual plant matter.

Another variation of no-till gardening is to lightly till. That means leaving the Rototiller in the garage and manually turning just the top inch or two (2.5 to 5 centimetres) of soil and residual plant matter using a fork or hoe. Although this isn't as safe as not tilling at all, the shallow disturbance is thought to be better for soil health than regular tilling.

Of course, the decision to till or not to till is firmly in the individual gardener's hands.[2]—SN

After a long winter, this crocus has popped up out of an insulating, protective layer of leaf mulch.

Why is mulching important in the garden?

The list of benefits of mulching is long, which is why, if you aren't already, you should seriously consider using it.

Mulch can suppress weeds by blocking the sunlight some weed seeds need to germinate. If the mulch layer is thick, the weeds will have a hard time breaking through it.

Mulch can protect the soil from wind erosion.

On hot days, mulch can keep moisture in the ground, instead of losing it to evaporation. This minimizes drought stress in plants. That lack of evaporation if your soil is sporting a layer of mulch? It also means your soil temperatures stay a bit cooler in summer.

In the winter, mulch can mitigate damage from freeze-and-thaw cycles by acting as insulation.

Organic mulches will naturally decompose over time, which means they can also feed the soil microbes, helping to keep the soil food web going.

Heavy rains can cause soil compaction and promote leaching of nutrients from the soil. Mulch can prevent that from occurring. Use of mulch can also minimize the risk of splashback onto plant foliage during rainfall or from supplemental irrigation. This reduces the chances of soilborne pathogens ending up on the leaves where they can infect the plant.

There are a couple of things to consider when choosing a mulch for your garden: aesthetics and your budget (see pages 112–122 for the various options). You need to love the way the mulch complements your plants and the style of your landscape. Certain types of mulch, such as rock, can be expensive, so if you're concerned about cost, source more economical choices.[3] —SN

How much mulch should I apply to my vegetable beds, to my flower beds, and beneath my trees and shrubs?

Mulch is meant to provide a layer of protection over the soil. It is not meant to bury the soil.

As with many things pertaining to gardening, we gardeners tend to think that if a bit is good, then more must be better. That really only applies to expanding your gardening footprint!

The mulch we apply should only be deep enough to do the job. Too little and it won't convey the benefits intended. The real problem is when we layer on mulch too deeply. That thick layer impedes both air and moisture from reaching the soil surface, leading to suffocation of roots and soil life. A thick blanket can overheat the soil. While that works in the winter when the mulch moderates soil temperature and prevents a freeze-and-thaw cycle from impacting the soil, it is too much of a good thing during the heat of the summer. Too much mulch ends up around plant stems and trunks, which can cause them to rot, especially if the mulch is moist. The deeper-than-needed mulch can also attract undesirable insects, slugs and/or snails, and small rodents who love the home we have created for them. In particular, those volcanoes we see mounded up around the trunks of trees are highly damaging. I once removed a foot of mulch from around a spruce, and it left a very distinct "ring around the tub" mark as testimony of too much of a good thing!

The optimum depth of mulch depends on the materials being used and what sort of garden bed it is helping. As a very general rule, two inches (five centimetres) should be the maximum depth for most garden beds. If the material is chunky, such as wood chips, then it can be a little thicker as the material is able to let air and water percolate through readily. Finer and denser materials, like montane mulch or grass clippings, should be around 1 inch (2.5 centimetres) as they are less able to allow moisture and air through. If the material is really lightweight and fluffy, such as straw, then the layer can be quite a bit thicker, say up to four inches (ten centimetres), as it will compact down quickly. Burlap and other densely woven materials that are only ¼ to ½ inch (0.6 to 1.25 centimetres) thick

This delightful combination of pansies and strawberry
plants is mulched with a layer of clean, weed-free straw.

are perfectly suited to annual beds and do the job magnificently. You only have to lift it up to check underneath to see that moisture is being kept in the soil and not heading into the air. Also, it will certainly deter weeds.

In my perennial beds I have taken to leaving small patches almost bare, with just a scattering of mulch, so that insects burrowing into the soil to create their nests have an easy entrance. The result? I have noticed a surge in bee populations in the past few years, along with other insects scurrying around.

We recommend you experiment with varying depths using different mulches to see what the optimum depth for your garden beds should be. Location, especially wind and exposure to direct sun, can make a real difference as to how much you should be using. If in doubt, go lightly. You can always add more.[4] —JM

Are cocoa bean shells toxic to pets?
Is it a useful mulch?

Cocoa bean mulch has a few very positive things going for it. First, it smells amazing when you apply it, and it doesn't immediately lose that yummy chocolate smell. More importantly (because no one actually *needs* a mulch that smells like chocolate, it's just nice), the colour—a dark, almost shiny brown—doesn't fade easily over time.

Most pets are unlikely to munch on cocoa bean mulch, although I have met some dogs that will eat anything! Cocoa bean mulch does contain the chemicals theobromine and caffeine, which, depending on how much is ingested, can be harmful to dogs and cats. Applications of high heat to the mulch will remove the cocoa fat from the shells but will not change the chemical composition. However, your pet would have to eat a large quantity of the mulch to get sick from it, and the hard shells presumably wouldn't be terribly appealing after the first mouthful, but as I mentioned before, I have met dogs who will devour pretty much anything that smells appealing. If you are worried about your pet's possible interactions with this type of mulch, don't apply it to your garden. Another factor to consider: cocoa bean mulch is fairly lightweight, and if it is dry, it can actually be lifted by high winds.[5]—SN

Cocoa bean mulch should be reserved for gardens that pets don't have access to. (Photo courtesy of Anne Bury)

What are the various types of wood mulches? Can they be used in all areas of the garden?

Arborist wood and bark chips are not the types of mulches to use in your vegetable garden or annual beds; put them at the bases of your trees and shrubs instead. There is a good reason for this: due to their high carbon-to-nitrogen ratio, wood mulches tend to temporarily tie up nitrogen right at the soil's surface where it meets the base layer of mulch. While this doesn't really affect trees and shrubs, which can handle the competition, it could be a serious problem if you use this type of mulch with annual plants. If you're worried about the effects of using wood and bark chips as mulch, dress the soil with a thin layer (about 1 inch or 2.5 centimetres) of compost before adding the wood chips. These chunky, bulky mulches are excellent at absorbing and holding moisture at the base of the plants.

Arborist wood chips are composed of mixed bark and wood leftover from tree removal and trimming; the chips are not all uniform in size and decompose at different rates (albeit slowly!). They are often available free of charge from arborists working in your area, so they're about as easy on the wallet as you can get. It is recommended to allow fresh arborist wood chips to sit for a few months before using them on beds or pathways as they can get pretty hot. You don't want steaming piles of wood near your plants.

These weathered wood chips are suitable for mulching this cotoneaster shrub.

Sawdust can be an inexpensive option to use as a mulch in a vegetable garden.

Bark mulch is made by scraping bark off trees that have fallen or been cut down. It can be purchased in bags or in bulk, and it's sometimes difficult to know where the bark has come from. It may also be more expensive than arborist wood chips, but bark mulch is very attractive, so the extra cost may be worth it. The pieces are usually roughly the same size.[6]

Sawdust is another mulch that may be better suited to woody perennials than annual plants, but one of my neighbours at my community garden uses it faithfully every year for his vegetables. Just like wood chips, sawdust can temporarily tie up nitrogen, so, if you choose to use it, add a layer of compost beneath it. Compared with straw and dried leaves, sawdust decomposes more slowly (but not as slowly as wood or bark chips). Go easy when you layer sawdust onto your soil: a 1-inch (2.5-centimetre) layer is enough. One drawback of sawdust is that it can easily compact. Also, be careful where you're sourcing your sawdust from; if it has been chemically treated, avoid using it.[7]—SN

I've heard that cedar chips will harm plants growing nearby. Is that true?

Cedar is well known as being the preferred wood for building raised beds and other structures as it takes a long time to rot. As a mulch it is also lightweight—fluffy almost—and smells terrific! However, the same properties that make it attractive as a building material can be detrimental when it is used as a mulch.

Cedar contains thujaplicin and thujone, chemicals that protect the wood by inhibiting bacteria and fungi. They also have insect-repelling properties, which together make for some powerful defences. (They also give cedar that lovely smell.) The downside is that those insect-repelling properties also discourage any beneficial insect, especially pollinators. The presence of these chemicals also ensures that cedar degrades much slower than most other mulches. Contrary to popular thinking, cedar does not have allelopathic properties to deter other plants growing nearby. It supresses weeds only because it is used as a mulch.

The bottom line is that cedar mulch is great for perennial beds but not where there are fruit-bearing plants. It would be excellent mulch if there is an insect infestation where you want populations to be knocked down. I am thinking my rose bushes and aphids here! I wouldn't use it for annual beds, both flowering and edible, where the soil is cultivated frequently. Those plants would be the most vulnerable to nitrogen deficiencies should the mulch end up being worked into the soil.[8]—JM

Is it safe to use mulch that has been dyed?

You don't have to worry about the dyes in coloured wood mulches: they are non-toxic. The dyes are either carbon-based or made from iron oxides, and they are safe to use in any garden application.

Now here is the clincher with dyed mulches: they are not usually composed of fresh bark chips, as the dyes do not readily adhere to them. Instead, recycled dry wood is often used, usually sourced from construction demolitions or shipping pallets. While this is a good way to recycle these waste products, it's important to make sure the wood has not been treated with chemicals (especially if you plan to use it in an edible garden). Finding out that information may require a phone call to the mulch manufacturer, as it likely won't be written on the bag, and the garden centre employees at the store you're purchasing it from won't be privy to that knowledge either. Bear in mind, Canada phased out the seriously toxic wood treatments, such as chromated copper arsenate, in 2004. If you're concerned, and you don't want to go to the trouble of researching the source of the wood, simply forgo the use of dyed mulches in organic gardens or when growing food.

One final note: dyed mulches do not typically retain their colour for a long period of time and will need to be replaced on a regular basis.[9] —SN

Dyed mulch can be an attractive short-term option, but we'd recommend it for ornamental plants instead of edible plants.

Should hay and straw be used as mulches for my garden? I've heard that they can contain a lot of weed seeds.

Straw is made up of the dry, often hollow stalks of grains, such as wheat, oats, and barley, after the good stuff (the grains) has been harvested. Because of this, there shouldn't be a lot of seed in straw, although occasionally the odd one will slip in. The grain most commonly used in North America for straw mulch is wheat.

Straw decomposes fairly rapidly, but it doesn't add a significant amount of organic matter to the soil as it breaks down. However, it is a clean, attractive mulch, useful between rows and plants. (Use a three- to six-inch or eight- to fifteen-centimetre layer, but do not nestle the mulch right up against the plants.)

If you don't want to hill potatoes (does anyone?), piling a mound of straw at the base of the plants does the trick just as well and it's far less work. Add straw to the hill as needed throughout the growing period.

Always ensure you use straw that has not been sprayed with herbicides or fire retardants, as the residuals will not be good for your plants.

Remember: mulches such as straw can be safe havens for insects, voles, and mice looking to hunker down for the winter. If it is not too labour intensive, remove the mulch late in the fall, just before freezing temperatures first occur, then place it back into position once the ground is frozen solid. This will prevent some of the critters from overwintering in the mulch and should still offer protection to your plants.

Hay has a bit of a bad reputation as a weed carrier, which isn't *always* warranted. Hay is composed of cut and dried legumes or grass (alfalfa is a popular type) and is often used as animal feed. Technically, hay should be cut before the seed heads appear, and if it is, you shouldn't have any problems with them sprouting in your garden. Proper timing of the cutting doesn't always occur, however, so unwanted seeds may pop up.

As it rapidly decomposes, hay becomes a good source of organic matter for the soil. It is also helpful in retaining soil moisture, although if it is applied in an overly thick layer and remains wet for a prolonged period of time, it can easily mould or rot.

Ruth Stout, a renowned early twentieth-century American organic farmer, advocated the use of a "permanent mulch," which would remain on the soil at all times, reducing the need to till. Weeding would be largely eliminated (that is, if the mulch itself didn't start up with volunteers of its own), and erosion and compaction would be minimized. Plants could be sown directly into the mulch, tucked into the soil beneath. This practice necessitates the use and expense of a large amount of hay (or straw, or a combination of the two), and the mulch must be repeatedly applied throughout the growing season. The benefits to the soil and to plant health are valid, however, and many gardeners today still employ similar techniques. A layer four to five inches (ten to thirteen centimetres) deep is what you should be aiming for. Before using hay, make sure it has not been grown using pesticides.[10] —SN

These young potato plants are happy surrounded by clean, weed-free straw mulch.

What about plant-based mulches such as dried leaves, grass clippings, and compost? Are they good mulches to use?

Ah, dried leaves . . . they are so very good as a mulch. They do all the things mulch should do, except perhaps provide an abundance of nutrition as they decompose (to address that, plop them in your compost bin with other wastes and let it all stew). Plus, they cost nothing!

Ideally, you'll want to shred them before you use them as mulch—if you have a lawn mower with a mulching blade, run it over the leaf pile a few times. Otherwise, just crumble them in your hands before laying them down overtop of the soil.

Use a two-inch (five-centimetre) layer of leaf mulch around the base of your trees and shrubs or herbaceous perennials. Pull the mulch back so that it isn't right up against the trunks or stems of plants.

If you have more dried leaves than you know what to do with, put them in your composter, but be careful not to upset the carbon-nitrogen ratio by adding too many at once. Or make leaf mould! (See page 63 for tips on how to do that.)

To prevent issues, don't use leaf mulch on lawns. A thick layer on turfgrass can actually harm the plants by not allowing sunlight and oxygen to penetrate. Moisture will be trapped in the leaves, and the whole mess can lead to rot and dead grass.

Also, don't use leaves from diseased trees as mulch.

Grass clippings are another easy-to-source mulch for your garden. If you collect the clippings after your lawn gets a trimming, you now have an inexpensive (read: free!) mulch for your garden.

Like other mulches derived from organic matter, grass clippings give back some nutrients to the soil as they decompose. They can also help retain soil moisture, and they might block the growth of some weeds as sunlight is less likely to penetrate the mulch.

*Grass clippings can be used in the
compost bin and as a mulch.*

Grass clippings can be problematic, however. If you use them fresh, be sure to apply only a very thin layer (about ¼-inch or six millimetres thick). Any more than that will tend to stay wet for prolonged periods and encourage rot, mould, and other diseases. The wet decomposing grass may also become extremely hot if the sun comes out, and the temperature could actually pose a health risk to nearby plants. (And the stench of rotting damp grass is a detriment in and of itself!) If you use herbicides on your lawn, or the weeds growing in it have gone to seed, you'll want to avoid altogether saving the clippings for use as a mulch.

It is better to dry the grass clippings first before applying them as a mulch. Find a spot (a concrete pad or paver is good) where you can lay them in the sun for a few days to dry out. If you do this, they can be safely used in a layer at least 1 to 2 inches (2.5 to 5 centimetres) thick. Try them in your veggie garden. They're not attractive enough to use in an ornamental garden, anyway. Remember, grass clippings decompose very rapidly and will need to be replaced often.[11]

Finally, we usually think of compost as a soil amendment rather than a mulch, but it can be very effectively used as both. A thick layer (about two inches or five centimetres) of compost around plants helps retain soil moisture, plus it has the huge added benefit of slowly releasing nutrients into the soil as it leaches downward with precipitation. (As it moves through the soil, it also enriches soil structure—another point in its favour.) It's also suitable for both vegetable and flower areas of your garden. Making your own compost is easy and economically viable (it's free!).

The biggest drawback with compost mulch is that you must continuously add it to garden beds throughout the growing season, as it is chewed up and ploughed through by microbes and other beneficial soil denizens. —SN

Is rock mulch suitable for all areas of the garden? What are my options?

There are many types of rock mulches to choose from. The most popular include:

* Lava rock: Yes, this is really lava from a volcano. It isn't heavy like most other rock types, and it has a rough, irregular shape and texture. It is red, brown, or black in colour.
* Pea gravel: This is the traditional gravel you may think of when you pave a driveway or a road. It is irregular in shape and can range from the size of a pea (surprising, I know!) to a golf ball. It is available in several colours, but many gardeners are attracted to the uniformity and "clean" look of white gravel.
* River rock: These are smooth, round stones (think of a riverbed and the tumbled rock that lines it). Found in a range of sizes, they are usually brown, tan, or grey in colour.

Rock mulches are attractive in many garden settings. They have long-lasting colour, and they don't ignite and burn easily like some other mulches. They can help prevent compaction and erosion of soils—a boon in windy sites or where water runoff is an issue.

Despite all its positive attributes, before selecting rock as a mulch, carefully consider how you plan to use it in your garden. If you need to transplant or sow plants on a regular basis, rock mulch is completely unsuitable. You won't want it for your vegetable or annual flower beds. Definitely save it for use around trees and shrubs or long-lived herbaceous perennials you don't plan to rehome any time soon. Although rock mulch won't necessarily eliminate weeds, it may weaken the roots, which may make unwanted plants easier to pull. Loose rocks can get into adjacent lawns, and may dangerously interfere with mowers. Rock mulch is inorganic and does not offer any nutrients to the soil. As the rock heats up in the sun, it can transmit the heat to the underlying soil. If you are trying to create a warmer microclimate in your garden, that might be useful, but hot soil isn't desirable in many cases. Due to its weight, handling and applying rock mulch is labour intensive. Depending on the source of the rock, it can also be a huge expense up front, but because you won't have to replace it often, the cost will eventually be recouped.[12] —SN

Do you recommend using black rubber mulch in any areas of my garden?

Let's get right to it: there are many pros and cons to using black rubber mulch. Here is our take.

The good:

* Making mulch from black rubber tires is a potential solution to the massive number of rubber tires requiring recycling in North America.
* Rubber is slower to decompose than most organic mulches. (Yes, it does eventually decompose, especially when certain types of bacteria begin to feed on it. It is not "permanent" as marketers of black rubber tire mulch would have you believe.)
* Rubber tire mulch retains its colour for a long period of time.

The bad:

* Rubber tire mulch can ignite, and once it begins burning, it can be tricky to stop it.
* The leachate (water that has percolated through) from decomposing rubber tires can contain several minerals that may not be beneficial to soil in large quantities. Research has shown that zinc toxicity, in particular, can be an issue.
* The plasticizers and accelerators used in the process of vulcanization for tires may be potential toxins.
* Rubber tire mulch can be harmful to aquatic wildlife.
* Some people will experience skin and eye irritation from exposure to rubber tire mulch. (I'm one of them.) I would highly recommend any other type of mulch instead.[13] —SN

What are cover crops and green manures, and how can they be used to help the soil and the plants in my garden?

Unlike crops grown to feed us or livestock, cover crops are grown to feed the soil with no intention to become food for our tables or for gardeners to collect seed to plant in the future.

The premise is based on the fact that where land is undisturbed, there is rarely soil without cover of some sort. That cover, whether it is weeds, grasses, meadows, or woodlands, protects the soil from erosion, be it from wind or hard rains causing runoff. Those rains are better captured where there are cover crops, with time to infiltrate the soil and avoid compaction. Cover cropping also acts to conserve organic matter, reduce carbon emissions, and moderate soil temperatures. Another benefit: since many cover crops are in the Fabaceae family, they fix nitrogen in the soil. They use nutrients to grow, preventing water-soluble ones from leaching out of the soil. Cover crops also reduce splashback from the soil onto the foliage of growing plants, lessening the chances of soilborne pathogens infecting the plants through wet leaves. Finally, cover crops provide habitat for many insects and other wildlife.

A cover crop becomes a green manure when it is cut down, either before or after it flowers, but before setting seed. It is then tilled into the soil to contribute its nutrients and biomass back to the soil. The biomass will quickly degrade, within two to three weeks depending on soil temperature, allowing for the garden to be sown or planted shortly afterward. A major benefit of using green manures is the addition of significant biomass, which over the years slowly improves soil's organic matter levels along with soil structure and texture. Not all of that biomass becomes OM; much is consumed by the activity of soil life as it goes about converting the biomass to plant-available nutrients, and a percentage is released from the soil as gases.

Those with large gardens may have the space to devote an entire season to a spring-sown cover crop, cutting it down and turning it back into the soil at the end of the season. The value of this approach is that the biomass generated will degrade over winter and its nutrients will be released into the soil, ready for planting next spring.

Fall rye is a quick-growing cover crop.

You can't go wrong using nitrogen-fixing legumes such as these field peas as a cover crop.

Most of us have smaller gardens to work with and need that space during the growing season for other uses. A winter-hardy species can be sown in the fall to germinate and establish roots and resume growing very early in the spring. Once it reaches four to six inches (ten to fifteen centimetres), it can be cut back and tilled into the top of the soil to degrade, leaving the rest of the season for other plants. Alternatively, a fast-growing spring-sown crop can be planted and then similarly turned in. Or cover crop plants can be sown in the margins of beds, between rows or blocks, and kept from going to seed by repeatedly being cropped back during the growing season with the clippings left on the soil to form mulch.

There is a wide variety of species that are favoured as cover crops, but they primarily fall into three categories: legumes, grains and grasses, and roots. Buckwheat is superb as an early-sown spring crop, as are field peas. Crimson clover, fava beans, and soybeans are excellent as all-season crops, and you likely will get some pods, too, for eating or some seed for next year. Fall rye, oats, and barley are all excellent choices for fall sowing, but choose ones most likely to overwinter in your area. Perennial cover crops, including Dutch white clover, hairy vetch, and alfalfa, are most suitable for pathways and planting around the edges of mounded beds.[14]—JM

"Soil is at the bottom of the food chain, yet it is the cornerstone of life on earth." — Unknown

We are just beginning to scratch the surface of all the complexities of soil and its wonderful relationships with the plants growing in our gardens. It's exciting to think what we'll learn next! — JM & SN

Acknowledgements

Janet and Sheryl would like to express our heartfelt thanks to the absolutely stellar publishing team at TouchWood Editions: Taryn Boyd and Tori Elliott (publisher and acting publisher), Kate Kennedy (editorial coordinator), Curtis Samuel (publicist and social media coordinator), Paula Marchese (copy editor), Meg Yamamoto (proofreader), Sydney Barnes (typesetter), and Pat Touchie (owner). A very special thank you goes out to designer Tree Abraham. We are so grateful for the opportunity we've been given to write these books!

Thank you also to Anne Bury, who generously contributed a photograph to the book.

We also want to let our wonderful readers know how much we appreciate their support and encouragement—it means the world to us!

From Janet:

My love affair with soil started with knowing that digging in it made me happy, but was well and truly ignited by the generosity of soil experts sharing their knowledge and research—most especially Kath Smyth, Mike Dorion, and Jeremy Zoller. Thank you all!

But I would be remiss in not acknowledging the forbearance of my family for all the soil I have tracked into the house over the years, along with soil samples and the odd insect (and worm) crawling around. Though the cats enjoy the fun!

And so many thanks to all the gardeners who love to get their hands in the soil and learn how to take care of it. Bless our grubby hands!

From Sheryl:

Unending love goes out to my husband, Rob, and my mum and dad and brother Derek.

I can't adequately express the gratitude and appreciation I have for the friendships of Angie and Paul, Lisa, Trina, Cori and Tony and family, Tina, and Kathy and Steve and family. Hugs and love to all of you!

Notes

Chapter One

1. Johnson, "Types of Organisms That Can Use Photosynthesis," Sciencing (website).

2. Ingham, "Soil Food Web," United States Department of Agriculture, Natural Resources Conservation Service.

3. Soil Food Web Institute (website), "What Makes a Healthy Soil Food Web?"

4. Lowenfels and Lewis, *Teaming with Microbes*, 19–27.

5. Ingham, "Soil Food Web," United States Department of Agriculture, Natural Resources Conservation Service; Cornell University, "Soil Organisms and Soil Ecology."

6. Thien, "Soil Triangle and Tests," University of Colorado at Boulder; Lerner, "What Is Loam?," Purdue University, Indiana Yard and Garden—Purdue Consumer Horticulture.

7. Pavlis, *Soil Science for Gardeners*, 109; Pavlis, "10 Easy Soil Testing Methods," Garden Fundamentals (website); Government of Western Australia, Department of Primary Industries and Regional Development, "Estimating Soil Texture by Hand."

8. Jeffers, "Soil Texture Analysis: 'The Jar Test," Clemson Cooperative Extension, Home and Garden Information Center; Oregon State University Extension Service, "Mechanical Analysis of Soils 'The Jar Test.'"

9. Miessler, *Grow Your Soil*, 75; Lovell, "Four Ways to Identify Hardpan," Grainews (website).

10. Baveye and Wander, "The (Bio)Chemistry of Soil Humus and Humic Substances," *Frontiers in Environmental Science*.

11. Pavlis, "Humus Does Not Exist—Says New Study," Garden Myths (website).

12. Pavlis, "What Is Humus?," Garden Myths (website).

13. Magdoff, "Repairing the Soil Carbon Rift," *Monthly Review*.

14. Eash et al., *Soil Science Simplified*, 36–38.

15. Reid, *Improving Your Soil*, 164–81; Lickacz and Penny, "Soil Organic Matter," Government of Alberta, Agri-Facts.

16. Pavlis, *Soil Science for Gardeners*, 89–96; McNear, "The Rhizosphere—Roots, Soil, and Everything in Between," Nature Education Knowledge Project (website); Bakker et al., "The Rhizosphere Revisited," *Frontiers in Plant Science*; Efretuei, "The Rhizosphere," Permaculture Research Institute (website); Lowenfels and Lewis, "Plants Are in Control," *Pacific Horticulture*.

17. Chadwick, "Mycorrhizal Fungi," *Mother Earth News*; Pavlis, "Mycorrhizae Fungi Inoculant Products," Garden Myths (website).

18. Chadwick, "Mycorrhizal Fungi and Plant Roots," *Mother Earth News*; Pace, "Hidden Partners: Mycorrhizal Fungi and Plants," New York Botanical Garden (website); Vinje, "Mycorrhizae Benefits," Planet Natural Research Center (website); Lowenfels and Lewis, *Teaming with Microbes*, 164–71; Reid, *Improving Your Soil*, 178–81.

19. Gonzaga, "Earthworm Invaders Alter Northern Forests," EarthSky (website); Miessler, *Grow Your Soil*, 67; Cordell, *Stay Grounded*, 17–20; Pavlis, "Vermicompost— Is It Really That Great?," Garden Myths (website).

20. Van Es, "Crop Rotation and Soil Tilth," Sustainable Agriculture Research and Education (website).

21. Curell, "Why Is Soil Water Holding Capacity Important?," Michigan State University Extension.

22. Perry, "pH for the Garden," University of Vermont Extension, Department of Plant and Soil Science.

23. Laqua Horiba (website), "Soil pH and Nutrient Availability."

24. Walliser, "Soil pH and Why It Matters," Savvy Gardening (website); Pavlis, *Soil Science for Gardeners*, 25–26; Eash et al., *Soil Science Simplified*, 69–74, 151–55.

25. Longstroth, "Lowering the Soil pH with Sulfur," Michigan State University Extension; Kluepfel and Lippert, "Changing the pH of Your Soil," Clemson Cooperative Extension, Home and Garden Information Center.

26. Reid, *Improving Your Soil*, 211–31; Lowenfels and Lewis, *Teaming with Microbes*, 98–110; Miessler, *Grow Your Soil*, 88–95.

27. Reid, *Improving Your Soil*, 233–36; Lowenfels and Lewis, *Teaming with Microbes*, 169–78.

28. Koike et al., "Vegetable Diseases Caused by Soilborne Pathogens," University of California, Division of Agriculture and Natural Resources.

29. Kelley and Sellmer, "Making Soilless or Peat-Based Potting Media," Penn State Extension.

30. Currell, "Determining Soil Infiltration Rate," Michigan State University Extension; University of Wisconsin–Madison Arboretum, "Infiltration Test: Exploring the Flow of Water Through Soils"; Kerby, "The Average Percolation Rate for Various Soil Types," Hunker (website).

31. Government of Manitoba, Agriculture, "Soil Management Guide: Soil Salinity"; Degnan, "How to Get Rid of Salt Accumulation on a Potted Plant," SFGate (website); Government of Alberta, Agri-Facts, "Dryland Saline Seeps: Types and Causes."

32. Pavlis, "Tighty Whitie Soil Test—A Brief Review," Garden Fundamentals (website); South Dakota Soil Health Coalition (website), "Soil Microbiology—'Tighty Whities' Test."

Chapter Two

1. Pavlis, *Soil Science for Gardeners*, 79–83; Hu, "Composting 101," Natural Resources Defense Council (website); Compost Education Center (website), "Hot Composting"; Solana Center for Environmental Innovation (website), "Passive or Active Composting: Which Is Right for You?"

2. Stone, "Simple Composting Methods," *Mother Earth News*; Vanderlinden, "Easy Composting: The Dig and Drop Method," The Spruce (website); LaVolpe, "Trench Composting with Kitchen Scraps," Farmers' Almanac (website).

3. Planet Natural Research Center (website), "Carbon-to-Nitrogen Ratios"; Brooklyn Botanic Garden, *Easy Compost*, 23, 25.

4. Brooklyn Botanic Garden, *Easy Compost*, 19–24.

5. The Rhubarb Compendium (website), "Composting Rhubarb Leaves"; Pavlis, "Will Oxalic Acid in Rhubarb Leaves Harm You?," Garden Myths (website).

6. Miessler, *Grow Your Soil*, 119–20.

7. Brooklyn Botanic Garden, *Easy Compost*, 41.

8. The Compost Gardener (website), "Ants in the Compost Pile."

9. Vanderlinden, "How to Make and Use Leaf Mold," The Spruce (website); Mills, "How to Make Leaf Mold Compost and Tips for Using It," Homestead Acres (website).

Chapter Three

1. Byju's Classes (website), "Difference between Organic and Inorganic Compounds."

2. Chicago Botanic Garden (website), "Synthetic vs. Natural Fertilizer"; Eco Organic Farm (website), "Comparing Organic and Inorganic Fertilizers? Which Is Better?"

3. Reid, *Improving Your Soil*, 232; Pavlis, "Fertilizer NPK Ratios—What Do They Really Mean?," Garden Myths (website).

4. Iannotti, "How to Improve Garden Soil with Amendments," The Spruce (website); Flowers, "How to Amend Garden Soil for Next Season," *Canadian Living*; Troy-Bilt (website), "Benefits of Amending Soil in the Fall."

5. Solomon, *The Intelligent Gardener*, 115; Albert, "Fertilizer Side-Dressing Vegetable Crops," Harvest to Table (website); Nardozzi, "How to Side-Dress Your Vegetable Garden," Dummies (website).

6. The Exploratorium (website), "Anatomy of an Egg"; Pavlis, "Eggshells—How Not to Use Them in the Garden," Garden Myths (website); Schwarcz, "Do Egg Shells Prevent Slug and Snails from Eating My Plants?," McGill University Office for Science and Society.

7. Zimmer, "How Caffeine Evolved to Help Plants Survive and Help People Wake Up," *New York Times.*

8. Rhoades, "Composting with Coffee Grounds—Used Coffee Grounds for Gardening," Gardening Know How (website); Hamer, "Whatever You Do, Don't Put Coffee Grounds in Your Garden," Discovery (website); Pavlis, "Getting Rid of Slugs with Coffee Grounds," Garden Myths (website).

9. Harris, "Differences between Cow Manure and Steer Manure," SFGate (website); Macdonald, "The Poop on Manure," West Coast Seeds (website); Mahr, "Using Manure in the Home Garden," University of Wisconsin–Madison Horticulture Division of Extension.

10. Pavlis, "Epsom Salt Myths in the Garden," Garden Myths (website).

11. Hodgson, "Banana Peels for Roses: Pretty Much a Garden Myth," Laidback Gardener (website).

12. Trail, "The Truth about Peat Moss," *The Ecologist.*

13. Hall, "Coir," How Products Are Made (website).

14. Pavlis, "Is Coir an Eco-friendly Substitute for Peat Moss?," Garden Myths (website).

15. Gibson and Russell, "Peat Moss vs. Coco Coir: Which Should You Use?," Gardening Channel (website); Smyth, "What Are the Drawbacks and Problems with Coconut Mulch?," SFGate (website); Pavlis, *Soil Science for Gardeners*, 163–64.

16. Solomon, *The Intelligent Gardener*, 171–72; Boyles, "How to Use Wood Ashes in the Home and Garden," *The Old Farmer's Almanac*; Iannotti, "Is Wood Ash Good for Garden Soil?," The Spruce (website).

17. Chalker-Scott, "The Myth of Gypsum Magic," Washington State University Puyallup Research and Extension Center.

18. Espiritu, "Perlite: What It Is and How to Use It in Your Garden," Epic Gardening (website).

19. Vermiculite.org (website), "Frequently Asked Questions"; Canadian Centre for Occupational Health and Safety, "Vermiculite Insulation Containing Asbestos," Government of Canada.

20. Grant, "What Is Zeolite: How to Add Zeolite to Your Soil," Gardening Know How (website).

21. KMI Zeolite (website), "Natural Zeolite Is a Powerful Natural Zeolite."

22. Garden Retreat (website), "How to Use Zeolite."

23. Cloninger, "6 Reasons You Should Be Using Wool Pellets in Your Garden Soil," Wild Valley Farms (website).

24. Affeldt, "Building Soil Health with Volcanic Basalt," Eco Farming Daily (website).

25. Pavlis, "Rock Dust—Can It Remineralize the Earth?," Garden Myths (website); Galvin and Lamp'l, "The Most Important Soil Amendment No One Ever Talks About," Growing a Greener World (website).

26. Chalker-Scott, "The Myth of Beneficial Bone Meal," Washington State University Puyallup Research and Extension Center.

27. Hodgson, "Bone Meal: Much Ado about Nothing," Laidback Gardener (website).

28. Smith, "Bone Meal vs. Blood Meal. What's the Difference?"; University of Connecticut Cooperative Extension System, "Soil Nutrient Analysis Laboratory"; Espiritu, "How to Use Blood Meal to Improve Your Soil," Epic Gardening (website).

29. Espiritu, "Feather Meal: A High-Nitrogen Organic Fertilizer," Epic Gardening (website).

30. Appelhof and Olszewski, *Worms Eat My Garbage*, 110, 113–15.

31. Brady, "How to Use Alfalfa Meal as a Soil Amendment and Compost Activator," Redbud Soil Company (website); Naeem, "Triacontanol: A Potent Plant Growth Regulator in Agriculture," Taylor and Francis Online (website); West Coast Seeds (website), "Alfalfa Meal 3-0-3."

32. Pavlis, "Fish Fertilizer—Is It Worth Buying?," Garden Myths (website).

33. Damrosch, "Why You Should Prepare a Seafood Dinner for Your Soil," *Washington Post*; Inrae Cirad Afz (website), "Shrimp Meal."

34. Osugi and Sakakibara, "How Do Plants Respond to Cytokinins and What Is Their Importance?," BMC Biology (website).

35. Grant, "What Is Glauconite Greensand: Tips for Using Greensand in Gardens," Gardening Know How (website).

36. Nielsen, "Mushroom Composting: What It Is, What It Does, and How to Make It," Epic Gardening (website).

37. Macdonald, "Lime Aid," West Coast Seeds (website).

Chapter Four

1. Reid and Wong, "Soil, Bacteria, and Fungi—New South Wales," Soil Quality (website); Voyle and Hudson, "What to Do about Compacted Soil," Michigan State University Extension.

2. Bernitz, "Low and No-Till Gardening," University of New Hampshire Cooperative Extension.

3. Compost Education Centre (website), "Mulching."

4. SFGate (website), "How Thick Should the Mulch Be in a Planting Bed?"; Sweetser, "How to Mulch Your Garden—Types of Mulch," *The Old Farmer's Almanac.*

5. Soloway, "Cocoa Bean Mulch Can Poison Dogs," Poison Control National Capital Poison Center (website).

6. Chalker-Scott, "Wood Chip Mulch: Landscape Boon or Bane?," Washington State University Puyallup Research and Extension Center.

7. Chalker-Scott, "Wood Chip Mulch: Landscape Boon or Bane?," Washington State University Puyallup Research and Extension Center.

8. Chalker-Scott, "Wood Chip Mulch: Landscape Boon or Bane?," Washington State University Puyallup Research and Extension Center; Palmer, "Properties of Hardwood and Cedar Mulch," SFGate (website); Baessler, "Shredded Cedar Mulch—Tips on Using Cedar Mulch in Gardens," Gardening Know How (website).

9. Ontario Urban Forest Council (website), "Beware of Toxic Mulch"; Government of Canada, "Staying Safe around Treated Wood."

10. Ellis, "Can You Mulch with Hay—Learn How to Mulch with Hay," Gardening Know How (website); MI Gardener (website), "These In-Ground Gardening Methods Will Transform Your Soil."

11. Grant, "Mulching with Grass Clippings: Can I Use Grass Clippings as Mulch in My Garden?," Gardening Know How (website).

12. Stone Arch (website), "Different Types of Landscaping Stones: How to Pick the Right One for Your Project."

13. RubberMulch.com (website), "The Pros and Cons of a Rubber Mulch Garden."

14. Pavlis, *Soil Science for Gardeners,* 126–28, 165–66; MacKenzie, "Cover Crops and Green Manures in Home Gardens," University of Minnesota Extension; Macdonald, "Green Manure Cover Crops," West Coast Seeds (website); Eisen, "Cross Canada Green Manure Use on Organic Vegetable Farms," Dalhousie University, Organic

Agriculture Centre of Canada; Wetherbee, "Grow Your Own Green Manure Cover Crop," *Mother Earth News*; Dyer, "Difference between Green Manures and Cover Crops," Gardening Know How (website).

Sources

Affeldt, Rich. "Building Soil Health with Volcanic Basalt." Eco Farming Daily (website). Accessed May 15, 2021. ecofarmingdaily.com/build-soil/building-soil-with -volcanic-basalt/.

Albert, Steve. "Fertilizer Side-Dressing Vegetable Crops." Harvest to Table (website). Accessed May 15, 2021. harvesttotable.com/side-dressing_vegetable_crops/.

Appelhof, Mary, and Joanne Olszewski. *Worms Eat My Garbage: How to Set Up and Maintain a Worm Composting System*. 35th anniversary ed. North Adams, MA: Storey Publishing, 2017.

Baessler, Liz. "Shredded Cedar Mulch — Tips on Using Cedar Mulch in Gardens." Gardening Know How (website). Last updated May 29, 2021. gardeningknowhow.com /garden-how-to/mulch/cedar-mulch-in-gardens.htm.

Bakker, Peter A.H.M., Roeland L. Berendsen, Rogier F. Doornbos, Paul C.A. Wintermans, and Corné M.J. Pieterse. "The Rhizosphere Revisited: Root Microbiomics." *Frontiers in Plant Science*. May 30, 2013. frontiersin.org /articles/10.3389/fpls.2013.00165/full.

Baveye, Philippe C., and Michelle Wander. "The (Bio)Chemistry of Soil Humus and Humic Substances: Why Is the 'New View' Still Considered Novel after More Than 80 Years?" *Frontiers in Environmental Science*. March 6, 2019. frontiersin.org /articles/10.3389/fenvs.2019.00027/full.

Bernitz, Nate. "Low and No-Till Gardening." University of New Hampshire Cooperative Extension. October 16, 2020. extension.unh.edu/blog/low-and-no-till -gardening.

Boyles, Margaret. "How to Use Wood Ashes in the Home and Garden: 5 Practical Uses for Wood Ash." *The Old Farmer's Almanac*. October 13, 2019. almanac.com /how-use-wood-ashes-home-and-garden.

Brady, Chris. "How to Use Alfalfa Meal as a Soil Amendment and Compost Activator." Redbud Soil Company (website). March 12, 2020. redbudsoilcompany.com/blogs/the -redbud-blog/how-to-use-alfalfa-meal-as-a-soil-amendment-compost-activator.

Brooklyn Botanic Garden. *Easy Compost: The Secrets to Great Soil and Spectacular Plants*. New York: Brooklyn Botanic Garden, 1998. bbg.org/gardening/handbook /easy_compost.

Byju's Classes (website). "Difference between Organic and Inorganic Compounds." Accessed May 15, 2021. byjus.com/chemistry/difference-between-organic-and -inorganic-compounds/#:~:text=The%20primary%20difference%20that%20 lies,simple%20C%2DH%20bond%20in%20them.

Canadian Centre for Occupational Health and Safety. "Vermiculite Insulation Containing Asbestos." Government of Canada. ccohs.ca/oshanswers/diseases /vermiculite.html#:~:text=Vermiculite%20produced%20by%20the%20Libby,may%20 be%20contaminated%20with%20asbestos.

Chadwick, Douglas. "Mycorrhizal Fungi and Plant Roots: A Symbiotic Relationship." *Mother Earth News.* August/September 2014. motherearthnews.com/nature -and-environment/nature/symbiotic-relationship-zm0z14aszkin.

———. "Mycorrhizal Fungi: The Amazing Underground Secret to a Better Garden." *Mother Earth News.* August/September 2014. motherearthnews.com/organic-gardening /gardening-techniques/mycorrhizal-fungi-zm0z14aszkin.

Chalker-Scott, Linda. "The Myth of Beneficial Bone Meal: Add a Handful of Bone Meal to Planting Holes before Installing Trees and Shrubs." Washington State University Puyallup Research and Extension Center. Accessed May 15, 2021. s3.wp .wsu.edu/uploads/sites/403/2015/03/bonemeal.pdf.

———. "The Myth of Gypsum Magic: Adding Gypsum to Your Yard or Garden Will Improve Soil Tilth and Plant Health." Washington State University Puyallup Research and Extension Center. Accessed May 15, 2021. s3.wp.wsu.edu/uploads/sites/403/2015 /03/gypsum.pdf.

———. "Wood Chip Mulch: Landscape Boon or Bane?" Washington State University Puyallup Research and Extension Center. First published via MasterGardenerOnline .com. Summer 2007. s3.wp.wsu.edu/uploads/sites/403/2015/03/wood-chips.pdf.

Chicago Botanic Garden (website). "Synthetic vs. Natural Fertilizer." Accessed May 15, 2021. chicagobotanic.org/plantinfo/faq/synthetic_vs_natural_fertilizer#:~:text=Natural %20fertilizers%20are%20organic%20products,%2Dderived%20or%20animal %2Dderived.&text=Synthetic%20fertilizers%20are%20those%20composed ,of%20nitrogen%2C%20phosphorus%20and%20potassium.

Cloninger, Cindy. "6 Reasons You Should Be Using Wool Pellets in Your Garden Soil." Wild Valley Farms (website). March 21, 2017. wildvalleyfarms.com/healthy-gardening -blog/6-reasons-you-should-be-using-wool-pellets-in-your-garden-soil.

Compost Education Centre (website). "Hot Composting." Accessed May 15, 2021. compost.bc.ca/wp-content/uploads/2015/03/4-Hot-Composting.pdf.

———. "Mulching." Accessed May 15, 2021. compost.bc.ca/wp-content/uploads /2015/03/7-Mulching.pdf.

Compost Gardener, The (website). "Ants in the Compost Pile." Accessed May 15, 2021. the-compost-gardener.com/ants-in-the-compost-pile.html#:~:text=When%20they%20 show%20up%20in,the%20pile%20is%20too%20dry.&text=The%20compost%20will%20 stop%20breaking,always%20the%20ants%20will%20relocate.

Cordell, Rosefiend. *Stay Grounded: Soil Building for Sustainable Gardens.* 2nd ed. Scotts Valley, CA: Create Space Independent Publishing, 2020.

Cornell University. "Soil Food Web: Soil Biology and the Landscape." Accessed October 17, 2021. css.cornell.edu/courses/260/Soil%20Eco%201.pdf.

Curell, Christina. "Determining Soil Infiltration Rate." Michigan State University Extension. September 19, 2016. canr.msu.edu/news/determining_soil_infiltration_rate.

———. "Why Is Soil Water Holding Capacity Important?" Michigan State University Extension. November 11, 2011. canr.msu.edu/news/why_is_soil_water_holding _capacity_important.

Damrosch, Barbara. "Why You Should Prepare a Seafood Dinner for Your Soil."
Washington Post. March 24, 2016. washingtonpost.com/lifestyle/home/from-seabed-to
-veggie-bed/2016/03/21/1733d8e4-ea08-11e5-bc08-3e03a5b41910_story.html.

Degnan, Sasha. "How to Get Rid of Salt Accumulation on a Potted Plant." SFGate
(website). Last updated April 23, 2021. homeguides.sfgate.com/rid-salt-accumulation
-potted-plant-22621.html.

Dyer, Mary H. "Difference between Green Manures and Cover Crops." Gardening
Know How (website). Last updated March 1, 2021. gardeningknowhow.com/edible
/grains/cover-crops/green-manure-vs-cover-crops.htm.

Eash, Neal S., Thomas J. Sauer, Deb O'Dell, and Evah Odoi. *Soil Science Simplified.*
6th ed. Hoboken, NJ: John Wiley & Sons, 2015.

Eco Organic Farm (website). "Comparing Organic and Inorganic Fertilizers? Which Is
Better?" ecoorganicfarm.com/2021/05/comparing-organic-and-inorganic.html.

Efretuei, Arit. "The Rhizosphere." Permaculture Research Institute (website).
November 11, 2016. permaculturenews.org/2016/11/11/the-rhizosphere/.

Eisen, Rochelle. "Cross Canada Green Manure Use on Organic Vegetable Farms."
Dalhousie University, Organic Agriculture Centre of Canada. August 2011. dal.ca
/faculty/agriculture/oacc/en-home/about/about-oacc/documents/newspaper-articles
/newsarticles-2011/newsarticle-2011-green-manure.html.

Ellis, Mary Ellen. "Can You Mulch with Hay—Learn How to Mulch with Hay."
Gardening Know How (website). Last updated July 18, 2020. gardeningknowhow.com
/garden-how-to/mulch/can-you-mulch-with-hay.htm#:~:text=Hay%20will%20not%20
give%20you,right%20over%20your%20garden%20soil.

Espiritu, Kevin. "Feather Meal: A High-Nitrogen Organic Fertilizer." Epic Gardening
(website). Last updated December 4, 2019. epicgardening.com/feather-meal/.

———. "How to Use Blood Meal to Improve Your Soil." Epic Gardening (website).
Last updated January 23, 2020. epicgardening.com/blood-meal/.

———. "Perlite: What It Is and How to Use It in Your Garden." Epic Gardening
(website). May 18, 2019. epicgardening.com/perlite/.

Exploratorium, The (website). "Anatomy of an Egg." Accessed May 15, 2021.
exploratorium.edu/cooking/eggs/eggcomposition.html.

Flowers, Frankie. "How to Amend Garden Soil for Next Season." *Canadian Living.*
September 25, 2012. canadianliving.com/home-and-garden/article/how-to-amend
-garden-soil-for-next-season.

Galvin, Ellen, and Joe Lamp'l. "The Most Important Soil Amendment No One
Ever Talks About." Growing a Greener World (website). Accessed May 15, 2021.
growingagreenerworld.com/rock-minerals-as-soil-amendments/.

Garden Retreat (website). "How to Use Zeolite." July 4, 2013. buyagreenhouse.com
/gardening-information/how-to-use-zeolite.

Gibson, Matt, and Erin Marisa Russell. "Peat Moss vs. Coco Coir: Which Should You
Use?" Gardening Channel (website). Accessed May 15, 2021. gardeningchannel.com
/peat-moss-vs-coco-coir-explained/.

Gonzaga, Shireen. "Earthworm Invaders Alter Northern Forests." EarthSky (website). September 13, 2016. earthsky.org/earth/european-earthworms-change-u-s-forests.

Government of Alberta, Agri-Facts. "Dryland Saline Seeps: Types and Causes." Last updated January 2000. open.alberta.ca/dataset/64384c8c-4d52-4e2c-bbf1-008bf82af440 /resource/08faaaba-9a92-4d7c-a1f8-d47b97a7b0cc/download/2000-518-12.pdf.

Government of Canada. "Staying Safe around Treated Wood." Last updated January 14, 2019. canada.ca/en/health-canada/services/consumer-product-safety/reports -publications/pesticides-pest-management/fact-sheets-other-resources/staying-safe -around-treated-wood.html.

Government of Manitoba, Agriculture. "Soil Management Guide: Soil Salinity." Accessed May 15, 2021. gov.mb.ca/agriculture/environment/soil-management/soil -management-guide/soil-salinity.html.

Government of Western Australia, Department of Primary Industries and Regional Development. "Estimating Soil Texture by Hand." Last updated November 16, 2020. agric.wa.gov.au/soil-constraints/soil-texture-estimating-hand.

Grant, Amy. "What Is Zeolite: How to Add Zeolite to Your Soil." Gardening Know How (website). Last updated November 6, 2019. gardeningknowhow.com/garden-how-to/soil -fertilizers/zeolite-soil-conditioner.htm.

Grant, Bonnie L. "Mulching with Grass Clippings: Can I Use Grass Clippings as Mulch in My Garden?" Gardening Know How (website). Last updated April 21, 2021. gardeningknowhow.com/garden-how-to/mulch/mulching-with-grass-clippings.htm.

———. "What Is Glauconite Greensand: Tips for Using Greensand in Gardens." Gardening Know How (website). Last updated January 22, 2021. gardeningknowhow .com/garden-how-to/soil-fertilizers/using-glauconite-greensand.htm.

Hall, Loretta. "Coir." How Products Are Made (website). Accessed May 15, 2021. madehow.com/Volume-6/Coir.html.

Hamer, Ashley. "Whatever You Do, Don't Put Coffee Grounds in Your Garden." Discovery (website). August 1, 2019. discovery.com/science/Coffee-Grounds-in-Your -Garden.

Harris, Rob. "Differences between Cow Manure and Steer Manure." SFGate (website). Accessed May 15, 2021. homeguides.sfgate.com/differences-between-cow -manure-steer-manure-103875.html.

Hodgson, Larry. "Banana Peels for Roses: Pretty Much a Garden Myth." Laidback Gardener (website). March 4, 2017. laidbackgardener.blog/2017/03/04/banana-peels -for-roses-pretty-much-a-garden-myth/.

———. "Bone Meal: Much Ado about Nothing." Laidback Gardener (website). April 14, 2018. laidbackgardener.blog/2018/04/14/bone-meal-much-ado-about-nothing/.

Hu, Sheila. "Composting 101." Natural Resources Defense Council (website). Accessed July 20, 2020. nrdc.org/stories/composting-101.

Iannotti, Marie. "How to Improve Garden Soil with Amendments." The Spruce (website). Last updated July 30, 2020. thespruce.com/making-good-soil-out-of-bad-1402428.

—————. "Is Wood Ash Good for Garden Soil?" The Spruce (website). Last updated May 15, 2020. thespruce.com/is-wood-ash-good-for-garden-soil-1403126#:~:text=Most %20wood%20ash%20contains%20a,can%20raise%20your%20soil%20pH.&text=Wood %20ash%20should%20also%20be,plants%20like%20rhododendrons%20and%20 blueberries.

Ingham, Elaine R. "Soil Food Web: Soil Biology and the Landscape." United States Department of Agriculture, Natural Resources Conservation Service. Accessed May 15, 2021. nrcs.usda.gov/wps/portal/nrcs/detailfull/soils/health/biology/?cid=nrcs142p2 _053868.

Inrae Cirad Afz (website). "Shrimp Meal." Accessed May 15, 2021. feedtables.com /content/shrimp-meal.

Jeffers, Andrew. "Soil Texture Analysis: The Jar Test." Clemson Cooperative Extension, Home and Garden Information Center. Last updated February 11, 2019. hgic.clemson .edu/factsheet/soil-texture-analysis-the-jar-test/.

Johnson, Doug. "Types of Organisms That Can Use Photosynthesis." Sciencing (website). Last updated April 19, 2018. sciencing.com/types-organisms-can-use -photosynthesis-7439559.html.

Kelley, Kathy, and Jim Sellmer. "Making Soilless or Peat-Based Potting Media." Penn State Extension. Last updated October 22, 2007. extension.psu.edu/homemade-potting -media#:~:text=A%20standard%20recipe%20for%20a,or%20vermiculite%20and%20 mix%20thoroughly.

Kerby, Kathryn. "The Average Percolation Rate for Various Soil Types." Hunker (website). Accessed May 15, 2021. hunker.com/13406958/the-average-percolation-rate -for-various-soil-types.

Kluepfel, Marjan, and Bob Lippert. "Changing the pH of Your Soil." Clemson Cooperative Extension, Home and Garden Information Center. Last updated October 20, 2012. hgic.clemson.edu/factsheet/changing-the-ph-of-your-soil/#:~:text=Aluminum %20sulfate%20will%20change%20the,the%20aid%20of%20soil%20bacteria.

KMI Zeolite (website). "Natural Zeolite Is a Powerful Natural Zeolite." Accessed May 15, 2021. kmizeolite.com/soil-amendment/.

Koike, Steven T., Krishna V. Subbarao, R. Michael Davis, and Thomas A. Turini, "Vegetable Diseases Caused by Soilborne Pathogens." University of California, Division of Agriculture and Natural Resources. 2003. anrcatalog.ucanr.edu/pdf/8099.pdf.

Laqua Horiba (website). "Soil pH and Nutrient Availability." Last updated September 22, 2015. horiba.com/en_en/applications/food-and-beverage/agriculture-crop-science /soil-ph-and-nutrient-availability/.

LaVolpe, Natalie. "Trench Composting with Kitchen Scraps." Farmers' Almanac (website). Last updated July 20, 2021. farmersalmanac.com/what-trench-composting -123957.

Lerner, Rosie. "What Is Loam?" Purdue University, Indiana Yard and Garden—Purdue Consumer Horticulture. Accessed May 15, 2021. purdue.edu/hla/sites/yardandgarden /what-is-loam/.

Lickacz, Jeremy, and D. Penny. "Soil Organic Matter." Government of Alberta, Agri-Facts. January 1985. www1.agric.gov.ab.ca/$department/deptdocs.nsf/all/agdex890/$file/536-1.pdf?OpenElement.

Longstroth, Mark. "Lowering the Soil pH with Sulfur." Michigan State University Extension. Accessed May 15, 2021. canr.msu.edu/uploads/files/Lowering_Soil_pH_with_Sulfur.pdf.

Lovell, Angela. "Four Ways to Identify Hardpan." Grainews (website). January 24, 2012. grainews.ca/features/four-ways-to-identify-hardpan/.

Lowenfels, Jeff, and Wayne Lewis. "Plants Are in Control." *Pacific Horticulture*. July 2006. pacifichorticulture.org/articles/plants-are-in-control/.

———. *Teaming with Microbes: The Organic Gardener's Guide to the Soil Food Web*. Rev. ed. Portland, OR: Timber Press, 2010.

Macdonald, Mark. "Green Manure Cover Crops." West Coast Seeds (website). August 10, 2020. westcoastseeds.com/blogs/garden-wisdom/green-manure-cover-crops.

———. "Lime Aid." West Coast Seeds (website). September 14, 2014. westcoastseeds.com/blogs/garden-wisdom/lime-aid#:~:text=Dolomite%20is%20most%20often%20used,soil%20nutrients%20into%20usable%20forms.

———. "The Poop on Manure." West Coast Seeds (website). January 24, 2021. westcoastseeds.com/blogs/garden-wisdom/poop-manure#:~:text=Horses%20digest%20their%20food%20less,of%200.5%2F0.3%2F0.4.

MacKenzie, Jill. "Cover Crops and Green Manures in Home Gardens." University of Minnesota Extension. Last updated 2018. extension.umn.edu/how-manage-soil-and-nutrients-home-gardens/cover-crops-and-green-manures.

Magdoff, Fred. "Repairing the Soil Carbon Rift." *Monthly Review*. April 1, 2021. monthlyreview.org/2021/04/01/repairing-the-soil-carbon-rift/.

Mahr, Susan. "Using Manure in the Home Garden." University of Wisconsin–Madison Horticulture Division of Extension. Accessed May 15, 2021. hort.extension.wisc.edu/articles/using-manure-in-the-home-garden/.

McNear, David H., Jr. "The Rhizosphere—Roots, Soil, and Everything in Between." Nature Education Knowledge Project (website). 2013. nature.com/scitable/knowledge/library/the-rhizosphere-roots-soil-and-67500617/.

Miessler, Diane. *Grow Your Soil: Harness the Power of the Soil Food Web to Create Your Best Garden Ever*. North Adams, MA: Storey Publishing, 2020.

MI Gardener (website). "These In-Ground Gardening Methods Will Transform Your Soil." Accessed May 1, 2021. migardener.com/these-in-ground-gardening-methods-will-transform-your-soil/.

Mills, Kim. "How to Make Leaf Mold Compost and Tips for Using It." Homestead Acres (website). Last updated December 3, 2020. homestead-acres.com/making-leaf-mold/.

Naeem, M. "Triacontanol: A Potent Plant Growth Regulator in Agriculture." Taylor and Francis Online (website). September 29, 2011. tandfonline.com/doi/full/10.1080/17429145.2011.619281.

Nardozzi, Charlie. "How to Side-Dress Your Vegetable Garden." Dummies (website). Accessed May 15, 2021. dummies.com/home-garden/gardening/vegetable-gardening /how-to-side-dress-your-vegetable-garden/.

Nielsen, Lorin. "Mushroom Compost: What It Is, What It Does, and How to Make It." Epic Gardening (website). Last updated March 18, 2019. epicgardening.com /mushroom-compost/.

Ontario Urban Forest Council (website). "Beware of Toxic Mulch." (Originally published as "Questions from You" by Ron Kujawski and Sonia Schloemann, *Hort News*, vol. 18, no. 5, UMass Extension.) June 7, 2014. oufc.org/2014/06/07/beware -toxic-mulch/.

Oregon State University Extension Service. "Mechanical Analysis of Soils 'The Jar Test.'" Accessed May 15, 2021. extension.oregonstate.edu/gardening/techniques /mechanical-analysis-soils-jar-test.

Osugi, Asami, and Hitoshi Sakakibara. "How Do Plants Respond to Cytokinins and What Is Their Importance?" BMC Biology (website). Accessed November 27, 2015. bmcbiol.biomedcentral.com/articles/10.1186/s12915-015-0214-5.

Pace, Matthew. "Hidden Partners: Mycorrhizal Fungi and Plants." New York Botanical Garden (website). Accessed May 15, 2021. sciweb.nybg.org/science2/hcol /mycorrhizae.asp.html.

Palmer, G.D. "Properties of Hardwood and Cedar Mulch." SFGate (website). Accessed May 15, 2021. homeguides.sfgate.com/properties-hardwood-cedar-mulch-48042.html.

Pavlis, Robert. "Eggshells—How Not to Use Them in the Garden." Garden Myths (website). Accessed May 15, 2021. gardenmyths.com/eggshells-not-use-garden.

⸻. "Epsom Salt Myths in the Garden." Garden Myths (website). Accessed May 15, 2021. gardenmyths.com/epsom-salt-for-plants/.

⸻. "Fertilizer NPK Ratios—What Do They Really Mean?" Garden Myths (website). Accessed May 15, 2021. gardenmyths.com/fertilizer-npk-ratios-what-do-they -really-mean/.

⸻. "Fish Fertilizer—Is It Worth Buying?" Garden Myths (website). Accessed May 15, 2021. gardenmyths.com/fish-fertilizer-worth-buying/.

⸻. "Getting Rid of Slugs with Coffee Grounds." Garden Myths (website). Accessed May 15, 2021. gardenmyths.com/getting-rid-slugs-coffee-grounds/.

⸻. "Humus Does Not Exist—Says New Study." Garden Myths (website). Accessed May 15, 2021. gardenmyths.com/humus-does-not-exist-says-new-study/.

⸻. "Is Coir an Eco-friendly Substitute for Peat Moss?" Garden Myths (website). Accessed May 15, 2021. gardenmyths.com/coir-ecofriendly-substitute-peat-moss /#more-4272 .

⸻. "Mycorrhizae Fungi Inoculant Products." Garden Myths (website). Accessed May 15, 2021. gardenmyths.com/mycorrhizae-fungi-inoculant-products/.

⸻. "Rock Dust—Can It Remineralize the Earth?" Garden Myths (website). Accessed May 15, 2021. gardenmyths.com/rock-dust-remineralize-earth/.

————. *Soil Science for Gardeners: Working with Nature to Build Soil Health.* Gabriola Island, BC: New Society Publishers, 2020.

————. "10 Easy Soil Testing Methods for Measuring Soil Health." Garden Fundamentals (website). Accessed May 15, 2021. gardenfundamentals.com/soil-testing -methods/.

————. "Tighty Whitie Soil Test—A Brief Review." Garden Fundamentals (website). Accessed May 15, 2021. gardenfundamentals.com/tighty-whitie-soil-test-review/.

————. "Vermicompost—Is It Really That Great?" Garden Myths (website). Accessed May 15, 2021. gardenmyths.com/vermicompost-is-it-great/.

————. "What Is Humus?" Garden Myths (website). Accessed May 15, 2021. gardenmyths.com/what-is-humus/.

————. "Will Oxalic Acid in Rhubarb Leaves Harm You?" Garden Myths (website). Accessed May 15, 2021. gardenmyths.com/oxalic-acid-rhubarb-leaves-harm-you/.

Perry, Leonard. "pH for the Garden." University of Vermont Extension, Department of Plant and Soil Science. Last updated 2003. pss.uvm.edu/ppp/pubs/oh34.htm.

Planet Natural Research Center (website). "Carbon-to-Nitrogen Ratios." Accessed May 15, 2021. planetnatural.com/composting-101/making/c-n-ratio/.

Reid, Greg, and Percy Wong. "Soil, Bacteria, and Fungi—New South Wales." Soil Quality (website). Last updated 2013. soilquality.org.au/factsheets/soil-bacteria-and-fungi-nsw.

Reid, Keith. *Improving Your Soil: A Practical Guide to Soil Management for the Serious Home Gardener.* Richmond Hill, ON: Firefly Books, 2014.

Rhoades, Heather. "Composting with Coffee Grounds—Used Coffee Grounds for Gardening." Gardening Know How (website). Last updated June 29, 2021. gardeningknowhow.com/composting/ingredients/coffee-grounds-gardening.htm.

Rhubarb Compendium, The (website). "Composting Rhubarb Leaves." March 23, 2019. rhubarbinfo.com/2019/03/composting-rhubarb.html.

RubberMulch.com (website). "The Pros and Cons of a Rubber Mulch Garden." Accessed May 15, 2021. rubbermulch.com/blogs/rubbermulch/31581761-the-pros-and -cons-of-a-rubber-mulch-garden.

Schwarcz, Joe. "Do Egg Shells Prevent Slugs and Snails from Eating My Plants?" McGill University Office for Science and Society. May 30, 2018. mcgill.ca/oss/article /you-asked/do-egg-shells-prevent-slugs-and-snails-eating-my-plants.

SFGate (website). "How Thick Should the Mulch Be in a Planting Bed?" Accessed May 20, 2021. homeguides.sfgate.com/thick-should-mulch-planting-bed-33045.html.

Smith, P. Allen. "Bone Meal vs. Blood Meal. What's the Difference?" Accessed May 15, 2021. pallensmith.com/2016/06/29/bone-meal-vs-blood-meal-whats-difference/.

Smyth, Danielle. "What Are the Drawbacks and Problems with Coconut Mulch?" SFGate (website). Last updated May 26, 2021. homeguides.sfgate.com/drawbacks -problems-coconut-mulch-48573.html.

Soil Food Web Institute (website). "What Makes a Healthy Soil Food Web?" Accessed May 15, 2021. soilfoodweb.com.au/about-our-organisation/benefits-of-a-healthy-soil-food-web.

Solana Center for Environmental Innovation (website). "Passive or Active Composting: Which Is Right for You? February 18, 2020. solanacenter.org/news/blog-posts/passive-or-active-composting-which-right-you.

Solomon, Steve. *The Intelligent Gardener: Growing Nutrient-Dense Food*. Gabriola Island, BC: New Society Publishers, 2013.

Soloway, Rose Ann Gould. "Cocoa Bean Mulch Can Poison Dogs." Poison Control National Capital Poison Center (website). Accessed May 15, 2021. poison.org /articles/cocoa-bean-mulch-can-poison-dogs#:~:text=Cocoa%20bean%20mulch%20 contains%20theobromine,is%20uncommon%20but%20has%20happened.

South Dakota Soil Health Coalition (website). "Soil Microbiology—'Tighty Whities' Test." January 2018. sdsoilhealthcoalition.org/wp-content/uploads/2020/01/Soil -Microbiology-Tighty-Whitie-Test-lesson-031918.pdf.

Stone, Pat. "Simple Composting Methods." *Mother Earth News*. July/August 1990. motherearthnews.com/organic-gardening/simple-composting-methods-zmaz90jazshe.

Stone Arch (website). "Different Types of Landscaping Stones: How to Pick the Right One for Your Project." Accessed May 15, 2021. stonearch.ca/different-types-of -landscaping-stones-how-to-pick-the-right-one-for-your-project/.

Sweetser, Robin. "How to Mulch Your Garden—Types of Mulch." *The Old Farmer's Almanac*. April 27, 2021. almanac.com/types-mulch-advantages-and-disadvantages -mulching.

Thien, Steve. "Soil Triangle and Tests: Estimating Soil Texture." Adapted by Dr. Timothy Kittel at University of Colorado at Boulder. Accessed May 15, 2021. culter .colorado.edu/~kittel/SoilTriangle&Tests_handout.pdf.

Trail, Jesse Vernon. "The Truth about Peat Moss." *The Ecologist*. January 25, 2013. theecologist.org/2013/jan/25/truth-about-peat-moss.

Troy-Bilt (website). "Benefits of Amending Soil in the Fall." Accessed May 15, 2021. troybilt.ca/en/knowledge-tb-how-to-amend-soil/knowledge-tb-how-to-amend-soil.html.

University of Connecticut Cooperative Extension System. "Soil Nutrient Analysis Laboratory." Accessed May 15, 2021. soiltest.uconn.edu/documents /fertilizerandgardenmeasurements2-5-15.pdf.

University of Wisconsin–Madison Arboretum. "Infiltration Test: Exploring the Flow of Water through Soils." April 5, 2015. arboretum.wisc.edu/content/uploads/2015/04 /RGS-2-4_Infiltration-Test.pdf.

Vanderlinden, Colleen. "Easy Composting: The Dig and Drop Method." The Spruce (website). Last updated May 27, 2019. thespruce.com/easy-composting-dig-and-drop -method-2539477.

———. "How to Make and Use Leaf Mold." The Spruce (website). Last updated June 29, 2021. thespruce.com/making-and-using-leaf-mold-2539475.

Van Es, Harold. "Crop Rotation and Soil Tilth." (Adapted from *Crop Rotation on Organic Farms: A Planning Manual* by Charles L. Mohler and Sue Ellen Johnson. College Park, MD: Sustainable Agriculture Research and Education, 2009.) Sustainable Agriculture Research and Education. Accessed May 15, 2021.

sare.org/publications/crop-rotation-on-organic-farms/physical-and-biological-processes
-in-crop-production/crop-rotation-and-soil-tilth/#:~:text=Tilth%20generally%20
refers%20to%20the,proliferation%2C%20allowing%20crops%20to%20thrive.

Vermiculite.org (website). "Frequently Asked Questions." August 2015. vermiculite.org
/wp-content/uploads/2014/09/FAQs.pdf.

Vinje, E. "Mycorrhizae Benefits." Planet Natural Research Center (website).
planetnatural.com/mighty-mycorrhiza/.

Voyle, Gretchen, and Hal Hudson. "What to Do about Compacted Soil." Michigan
State University Extension. February 21, 2014. canr.msu.edu/news/what_to_do_about
_compacted_soil.

Walliser, Jessica. "Soil pH and Why It Matters." Savvy Gardening (website). Accessed
May 15, 2021. savvygardening.com/soil-ph-and-why-it-matters/.

West Coast Seeds. "Alfalfa Meal 3-0-3." Accessed May 15, 2021. westcoastseeds
.com/products/alfalfa-meal-2#:~:text=Alfalfa%20Meal%20Fertilizer%20makes%20
an,%2D10kg%2F10%20square%20meters.

Wetherbee, Kris. "Grow Your Own Green Manure Cover Crop." *Mother Earth News.*
April/May 2020. motherearthnews.com/organic-gardening/green-manure-cover-crop
-zmaz00amzgoe.

Zimmer, Carl. "How Caffeine Evolved to Help Plants Survive and Help People Wake
Up." *New York Times.* September 4, 2014. nytimes.com/2014/09/04/science/how
-caffeine-evolved-to-help-plants-survive-and-help-people-wake-up.html.

Index

© Steve Melrose

About the Authors

SHERYL NORMANDEAU was born and raised in the Peace Country region of northern Alberta and has made Calgary her home since 1994. A writer and master gardener, Sheryl holds a bachelor's degree in English, as well as a Prairie Horticulture Certificate and an Urban Sustainable Agriculture Certificate. Since 2013, she has served as the online Ask an Expert for the Calgary Horticultural Society. She works at the Calgary Public Library—besides gardening, books of all kinds are her grand passion! She is a small-space gardener (on a tiny balcony and in a plot in a nearby community garden) and she is most enthusiastic about growing veggies. In addition to the Guides for the Prairie Gardener series, Sheryl is the author of the cookbook *The Little Prairie Book of Berries: Recipes for Saskatoons, Sea Buckthorn, Haskap Berries and More*. She lives with her husband, Rob, and their rescue cat Smudge. Find Sheryl at Flowery Prose (floweryprose .com) and on Facebook (@FloweryProse), Twitter (@Flowery_Prose), and Instagram (flowery_prose).

JANET MELROSE was born in Trinidad, West Indies, and immigrated to Canada in 1964. She has lived in Calgary since 1969. She is a master gardener and the creator and owner of the successful horticulture business Calgary's Cottage Gardener, which specializes in garden education and consultation, horticultural therapy, and advocating for sustainable local food systems. She holds bachelor's degrees in sociology and history, a Prairie Horticulture Certificate, and a Horticultural Therapy Certificate. Janet is a lifelong gardener, coming from a heritage of English gardening. She has a large garden at home in the suburbs of Calgary that can only be described as a typical cottage garden. She cares for eight other gardens throughout Calgary through her work as a horticultural therapist, as well as a bed at the Inglewood Community Garden. She is married to Steve and has two children, Jennifer and David. Three cats, Patrick, Theo, and Mia, currently own their home and patrol against the deer, hares, squirrels, skunk, mice, insects, and assorted birds that believe the garden is theirs, too! Connect with Janet on Facebook (@Calgarys-Cottage-Gardener), Twitter (@CalCottageGrdnr), and Instagram (CalgarysCottageGardener).

NOTES